Managing Editor

Mara Ellen Guckian

Editor in Chief

Karen J. Goldfluss, M.S. Ed.

Creative Director

Sarah M. Fournier

Cover Artist

Sarah Kim

Imaging

James Edward Grace

Publisher

Mary D. Smith, M.S. Ed.

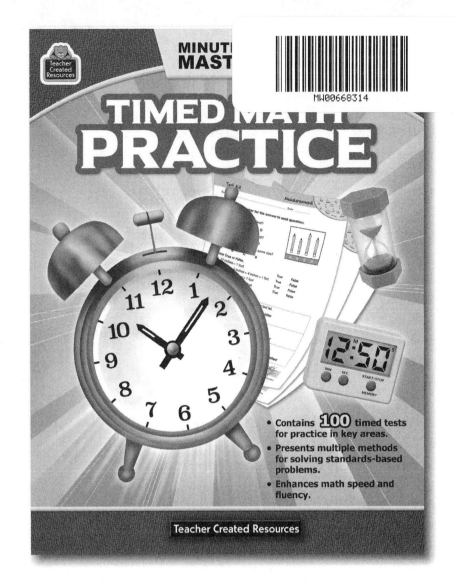

For correlations to the Common Core State Standards, see pages 105–106 of this book or visit *http://www.teachercreated.com/ standards/*.

Teacher Created Resources

12621 Western Avenue

Garden Grove, CA 92841

www.teachercreated.com

ISBN: 978-1-4206-8081-2

© 2017 Teacher Created Resources

Made in U.S.A.

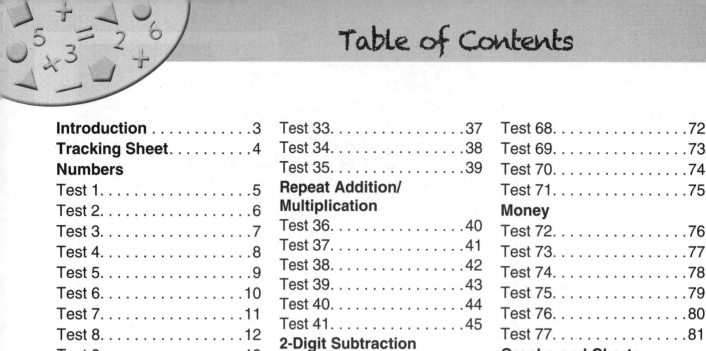

Table of Contents

Introduction

The *Minutes to Mastery* series was designed to help students build confidence in their math abilities during testing situations. As students develop fluency with math facts and operations, they improve their abilities to do different types of math problems comfortably and quickly.

Each of the 100 tests in this book has 10 questions in key math areas. Multiple opportunities are presented to solve the standards-based problems while developing speed and fluency. The pages present problems in a variety of ways using different terminology. For instance, in subtraction, students might be asked to *subtract* or to *find the difference*. Terms like *less* and *minus* are both used to ensure that students are comfortable with different phrasings. Word problems are included to provide additional practice decoding text for clues. Critical thinking and abstract reasoning play such an important role in solving math problems, and practice is imperative.

Keep in mind, timing can sometimes add to the stress of learning. If this is the case for your math learner(s), don't focus on timing in the beginning. As confidence in the process of answering a number of different types of questions builds, so will accuracy and speed. Then you can introduce timing.

Establish a timing system that works well for your group. Here are steps to help you get started:

1. Present a worksheet without officially timing it to get a sense of how long it will take to complete—perhaps 10 minutes. Ideally, you want all ten questions per page to be answered.

2. Allow students to practice using the preferred timer before taking a timed test.

3. Remind students to write their answers neatly.

4. Take a few timed tests and see how it works. Adjust the time as needed.

5. Work to improve the number of correct answers within the given time. Remind students that it is important to be accurate, not just fast!

6. Encourage students to try to do their best each time, to review their results, and to spend time working on areas where they had difficulties. The Tracking Sheet can be used to record the number of correct answers for each test. The final column can be used for the date the test was taken or for initials.

The section at the bottom of each page can be used to record specific progress on that test, including the time the student started the test, finished the test, the total time taken, how many problems were completed, and how many problems were correct.

Hopefully, with practice, all students will begin challenging themselves to go faster, while remaining accurate and writing clearly.

Name _____

Numbers		
Test 1	/10	
Test 2	/10	
Test 3	/10	
Test 4	/10	
Test 5	/10	
Test 6	/10	
Test 7	/10	
Test 8	/10	
Test 9	/10	
Operations in Base 10		
Test 10	/10	
Test 11	/10	
Test 12	/10	
Test 13	/10	
Test 14	/10	
Test 15	/10	
Greater Than, Less Than, Equal		
Test 16	/10	
Test 17	/10	
Test 18	/10	
Test 19	/10	
Test 20	/10	
Addition Sums to 20		
Test 21	/10	
Test 22	/10	
Test 23	/10	
Test 24	/10	
Test 25	/10	
2-Digit Addition		
Test 26	/10	
Test 27	/10	
Test 28	/10	
3-Digit Addition		
Test 29	/10	
Test 30	/10	
Addition with Regrouping		
Test 31	/10	
Test 32	/10	
Test 33	/10	
Test 34	/10	
Test 35	/10	

Repeat Addition/Multiplication		
Test 36	/10	
Test 37	/10	
Test 38	/10	
Test 39	/10	
Test 40	/10	
Test 41	/10	
2-Digit Subtraction		
Test 42	/10	
Test 43	/10	
Test 44	/10	
Test 45	/10	
Test 46	/10	
3-Digit Subtraction		
Test 47	/10	
Test 48	/10	
Test 49	/10	
Subtraction with Regrouping		
Test 50	/10	
Test 51	/10	
Test 52	/10	
Mixed Equations		
Test 53	/10	
Test 54	/10	
Test 55	/10	
Test 56	/10	
Measurement		
Test 57	/10	
Test 58	/10	
Test 59	/10	
Test 60	/10	
Test 61	/10	
Test 62	/10	
Test 63	/10	
Test 64	/10	
Test 65	/10	
Time		
Test 66	/10	
Test 67	/10	
Test 68	/10	
Test 69	/10	
Test 70	/10	
Test 71	/10	

Money		
Test 72	/10	
Test 73	/10	
Test 74	/10	
Test 75	/10	
Test 76	/10	
Test 77	/10	
Graphs and Charts		
Test 78	/10	
Test 79	/10	
Test 80	/10	
Test 81	/10	
Geometry		
Test 82	/10	
Test 83	/10	
Test 84	/10	
Test 85	/10	
Test 86	/10	
Test 87	/10	
Symmetry		
Test 88	/10	
Test 89	/10	
Test 90	/10	
Perimeter		
Test 91	/10	
Test 92	/10	
Test 93	/10	
Fractions		
Test 94	/10	
Test 95	/10	
Test 96	/10	
Test 97	/10	
Number Words		
Test 98	/10	
Test 99	/10	
Test 100	/10	

Name _____ Date _____

How many balls are in each row?

1.

2.

3.

4.

Write the number for each number word.

5. four _____ **6.** nine _____

7. seven _____ **8.** three _____

9. Circle the ball that is third in the row below.

10. Cross out the ball that is fifth in the row above.

Started:	Finished:	Total Time:	Completed:	Correct:

Name _____ Date _____

How many fruits are in each group?

1.

2.

3.

4.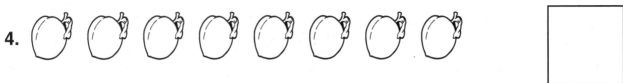

Write the missing number for each group of numbers.

5. 1, 2, _____, 4, 5   **6.** 2, 3, 4, 5, _____

7. 6, 7, _____, 9, 10   **8.** 2, 3, _____, 5, 6

Circle the correct number for each group of animals.

9.   **5**   **6**   **7**   **8**   **9**   **10**

10.   **5**   **6**   **7**   **8**   **9**   **10**

Started:	Finished:	Total Time:	Completed:	Correct:

Name _____　　Date _____

How many balls are in each group?

1. _____ ⬮⬮⬮⬮⬮⬮⬮⬮⬮⬮

2. _____ ⚾⚾⚾⚾⚾⚾⚾⚾⚾⚾⚾

3. _____ 🏀🏀🏀🏀🏀🏀🏀🏀

4. _____ ⚽⚽⚽⚽⚽⚽⚽⚽⚽

Write the number for each number word.

5. eight _____

6. eleven _____

7. nine _____

8. two_____

9. Circle the baseball that is tenth in the row.

10. Circle the bat that is ninth in the row.

Started:	Finished:	Total Time:	Completed:	Correct:

Name _____ Date _____

How many fruits are in each group?

1.

2.

3.

4.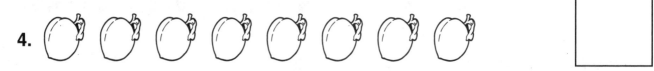

Write the missing number for each group of numbers.

5. 7, 8, _____, 10, 11   **6.** 9, 10, 11, _____, 13

7. 8, 9, _____, 11, 12   **8.** 6, 7, 8, _____, 10

Circle the correct number for each group of insects.

9.

  10   **11**   **12**   **13**   **14**   **15**

10.

  10   **11**   **12**   **13**   **14**   **15**

Started:	Finished:	Total Time:	Completed:	Correct:

Name _____ Date _____

Write the word for each number.

1. 13 _____

3. 15 _____

2. 14 _____

4. 16 _____

Write the amount for each group of items.

5.

6.

7.

Arrange the numbers in order from least to greatest.

8.

| 12 | 8 | 11 | 9 | 10 |

_____ _____ _____ _____ _____

9.

| 10 | 14 | 12 | 13 | 11 |

_____ _____ _____ _____ _____

10.

| 15 | 14 | 16 | 12 | 13 |

_____ _____ _____ _____ _____

| Started: | Finished: | Total Time: | Completed: | Correct: |

Name _____ Date _____

Write the word for each number.

1. 17 _____

2. 18 _____

3. 19 _____

4. 20 _____

Circle the correct number for each group of shells.

5.		15 20 18
6.		18 19 17
7.		14 15 16

Circle the *odd* numbers in each row.

8.   12   13   14   15   16   17   18

9.   20   16   13   19   14   11   15

10.   13   11   16   17   18   19   20

Started:	Finished:	Total Time:	Completed:	Correct:

Name _____ Date _____

Circle the *largest* number in each row.

1.	12	18	15	19	14	11
2.	20	16	13	14	17	10
3.	17	13	15	16	14	12

Write the number word for each group of stars.

4. ☆☆☆☆☆☆☆☆   _____

5. ☆☆☆☆☆☆☆
   ☆☆☆☆☆☆   _____

6. ☆☆☆☆☆☆☆☆☆
   ☆☆☆☆☆☆☆☆☆   _____

7. ☆☆☆☆☆☆☆☆
   ☆☆☆☆☆☆☆☆   _____

Circle the *even* numbers in each row.

8.	10	11	12	13	14	15	16
9.	20	16	13	19	14	11	15
10.	13	11	16	17	18	19	20

Started:	Finished:	Total Time:	Completed:	Correct:

Name _____ Date _____

Write the missing number for each number line.

1.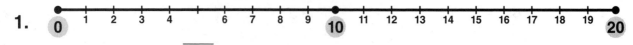

2.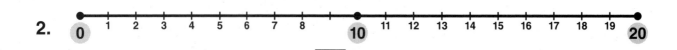

Look at the parade of dogs and answer the questions below.

A   B   C   D   E   F

3. Which dog is fourth? _____ 4. Which dog is first? _____

5. Which dog is sixth? _____ 6. Which dog is second? _____

7. Which dog is fifth? _____ 8. Which dog is third? _____

Write the missing number for each number line.

9.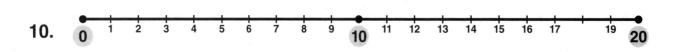

10.

Started:	Finished:	Total Time:	Completed:	Correct:

Name _____   Date _____

Solve the addition problems.

1. ☆☆☆☆ + ☆☆☆ = _____

2. ☆☆☆☆☆☆ + ☆☆ = _____

3. ☆☆☆☆☆ + ☆☆☆☆☆ = _____

Use the number lines to solve the problems.

4. $7 + 2 =$ _____   0 1 2 3 4 5 6 7 8 9 10

5. $2 + 4 =$ _____   0 1 2 3 4 5 6 7 8 9 10

6. $4 + 4 =$ _____   0 1 2 3 4 5 6 7 8 9 10

7. $12 + 3 =$ _____

8. $10 + 8 =$ _____

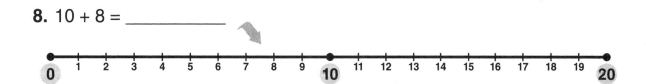

9. Write the number nineteen. _____

10. Write the number twelve. _____

Started:	Finished:	Total Time:	Completed:	Correct:

Name _____ Date _____

What number is shown in each set?

1. 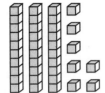   _____ tens _____ ones = _____

2. 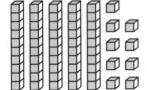   _____ tens _____ ones = _____

Which number is in the ones place in each number below?

3. 41 _____   **4.** 69 _____   **5.** 485 _____

Which number is in the tens place in each number below?

6. 32 _____

7. 56 _____

8. 104 _____

9. 398 _____

Circle the correct answer to the statement.

10. There are 77 cubes.   **True**   **False**

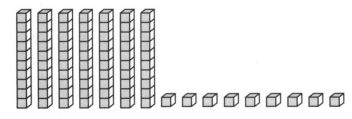

Started:	Finished:	Total Time:	Completed:	Correct:

Name _____   Date _____

Show the following numbers as tens and ones.

1. 22 = _____ tens _____ ones

2. 65 = _____ tens _____ ones

3. 49 = _____ tens _____ ones

Circle the correct number for each number word.

4. thirty-nine   **90**   **39**   **9**   **30**

5. sixty-five   **65**   **60**   **56**   **55**

Which answer shows 34?   **A** or **B**

6. **A.** 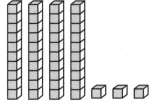   **B.**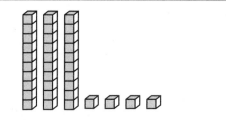

Solve the problems.

7. 10 + 20 + 30 = _____   **8.** 5 + 25 + 10 = _____

9. 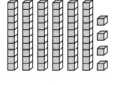 _____ tens _____ ones = _____

10. 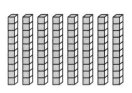 _____ tens _____ ones = _____

Started:	Finished:	Total Time:	Completed:	Correct:

Name _____ Date _____

Show the following numbers as hundreds, tens, and ones.

1. 246 = _____ hundreds _____ tens _____ ones

2. 891 = _____ hundreds _____ tens _____ ones

3. 552 = _____ hundreds _____ tens _____ ones

Choose the correct number words for each number.

4.	365	**A.** three hundred fifty-six	**B.** three hundred sixty-five
5.	121	**A.** one hundred twelve	**B.** one hundred twenty-one
6.	723	**A.** seven hundred twenty-three	**B.** seven hundred thirty-two

Which number is greater? Circle your answers.

7.   **A.** 498   **B.** 489

8.   **A.** 636   **B.** 663

How many hundreds, tens, and ones are shown in the base 10 blocks.

9.
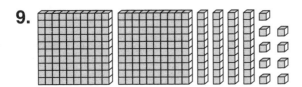

_____ hundreds _____ tens _____ ones

10.
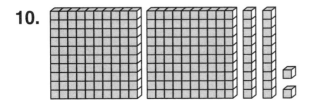

_____ hundreds _____ tens _____ ones

Started:	Finished:	Total Time:	Completed:	Correct:

Name _____   Date _____

Write the following as numbers.

1.

Hundreds	Tens	Ones
4	7	6

= _____

2.

Hundreds	Tens	Ones
6	9	3

= _____

3.

Hundreds	Tens	Ones
1	5	3

= _____

How many hundreds, tens, and ones are shown in the base 10 blocks.

4. 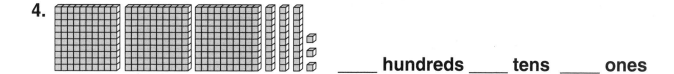 _____ hundreds _____ tens _____ ones

5.  _____ hundreds _____ tens _____ ones

Circle the correct number for each number word.

6. three hundred forty-nine   394   493   349   949

7. six hundred seventy-five   657   765   675   567

8. eight hundred twenty-four   842   482   428   824

Solve the problems.

9. 7 tens + 6 ones = _____   10. 200 + 300 = _____

Started:	Finished:	Total Time:	Completed:	Correct:

Name _____ Date _____

Look at the numbers in each circle. Arrange the numbers to make the largest number you can make. Write the number on the line.

1. (6 1 7) _____

2. (7 8 6) _____

3. (1 0 9) _____

4. (5 8 7) _____

Circle the number that is closest to 512.

5.   515   510   520

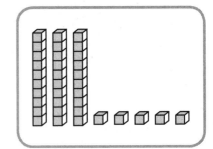

Use the base 10 blocks to answer the next four questions.

6. How many cubes are there? _____

7. How many more 10s do you need to make 65? _____

8. How many more ones do you need to make 39? _____

9. How many more 10s do you need to make 55? _____

Circle the correct answer for the unit cubes shown.

10. 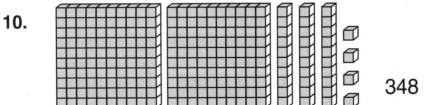   348   234   338

Started:	Finished:	Total Time:	Completed:	Correct:

Name _____ Date _____

What is the place value for each of the underlined numbers?

Hundreds	Tens	Ones

1. 3<u>7</u>5 _____

2. <u>5</u>43 _____

3. 82<u>1</u> _____

Write the numbers below in words. Don't forget the hyphens.

4. 854 _____

5. 108 _____

6. 396 _____

Use the numbers in the ovals to answer the questions below.

(760)   (386)   (441)   (809)   (624)   (190)

7. What number has a 4 in the *hundreds* place? _____

8. What number has a 6 in the *ones* place? _____

9. What number has a 2 in the *tens* place? _____

10. What number has a zero in the *tens* place? _____

Started:	Finished:	Total Time:	Completed:	Correct:

Name _____   Date _____

Answer *True* or *False* for each problem.

1.	443 > 434	**True**	**False**
2.	89 < 88	**True**	**False**
3.	64 > 46	**True**	**False**
4.	656 < 665	**True**	**False**

Look at the numbers below. Write a number that is 10 less on the first line. Write a number that is 10 more on the last line.

5. _____   (54)   _____

6. _____   (123)   _____

7. _____   (678)   _____

Fill in each oval with the correct symbol (>, <, or =).

8. 134 ( ) 143

9. 665 ( ) 656

10. 939 ( ) 939

Started:	Finished:	Total Time:	Completed:	Correct:

Name _____ Date _____

Compare the two sets of cubes. Write the totals and decide which symbol (>, <, or =) to use.

1.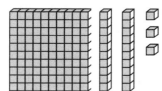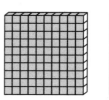

_____   _____

2.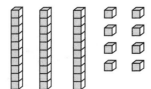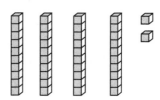

_____   _____

Answer *True* or *False* for each statement.

3. 74 = seventy-four	**True**	**False**
4. 49 > fifty	**True**	**False**
5. 223 < two hundred twenty-three	**True**	**False**
6. 12 = thirteen	**True**	**False**

Solve the addition problems and then fill each oval with the correct symbol (>, <, or =).

7. 7 + 5 ⬭ 5 + 7   **8.** 3 + 4 ⬭ 4 + 5

9. 4 + 5 ⬭ 5 + 5   **10.** 6 + 2 ⬭ 4 + 4

Started:	Finished:	Total Time:	Completed:	Correct:

Name _____ Date _____

Place the correct the symbol (>, <, or =) in each oval.

1. 11 + 5 ⬭ 17　　　　**2.** 8 + 4 ⬭ 12

3. 12 + 6 ⬭ 16　　　　**4.** 9 + 4 ⬭ 13

Answer the questions. Show your work.

| **5.** | Michael has one dozen eggs. Joe has 10 eggs.
Who has more eggs?

_____ has more eggs. | 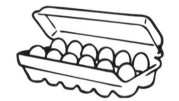 |

| **6.** | Sam has fifteen cars. Jake has fifty cars.
Who has more cars?

_____ has more cars. |  |

Fill in each oval with the correct symbol (>, <, or =).

7. 32 ⬭ 34　　　　**8.** 45 ⬭ 43

9. 776 ⬭ 767　　　　**10.** 101 ⬭ 101

| Started: | Finished: | Total Time: | Completed: | Correct: |

Name _____ Date _____

Place the correct the symbol (>, <, or =) in each oval.

1. 863 $\bigcirc$ 836   **2.** 472 $\bigcirc$ 427   **3.** 111 $\bigcirc$ 121

Write the problem using >, <, or = signs.

4. Kate has six balls and Elle has five balls.

_____ $\bigcirc$ _____

Answer the question.

5. In problem 4, who had more balls?

_____ had more balls.

Answer *True* or *False* for each statement.

6. 84 > eighty-five   **True**   **False**

7. forty seven = 47   **True**   **False**

Fill in each oval with the correct symbol (>, <, or =).

8.   4 + 5 $\bigcirc$ 3 + 7

9.   1 + 6 $\bigcirc$ 2 + 6

10.   3 + 5 $\bigcirc$ 5 + 3

Started:	Finished:	Total Time:	Completed:	Correct:

Name _____ Date _____

Look at each number below. Write a number that is 10 less before the number. Write a number that is 10 more after the number.

1. _____ (88) _____

2. _____ (156) _____

3. _____ (760) _____

4. _____ (910) _____

Solve. Fill in each oval with the correct symbol (>, <, or =).

5. 7 + 8 ( ) 18

6. 10 + 9 ( ) 19

7. 12 ( ) 9 + 4

8. 15 ( ) 5 + 8

Write a problem using >, <, or = signs. Then answer problem 10.

9. On Monday, there were twelve busses in the parking lot. On Tuesday, there were twenty busses in the lot.

_____ ( ) _____

10. In problem 9, which day had more busses?

There were more busses on _____.

Started:	Finished:	Total Time:	Completed:	Correct:

Name _____ Date _____

Find the sums.

1.   6
    + 3

2.   8
    + 2

Fill in the blank to solve the problems.

3. _____ + 6 = 14

4. 3 + _____ = 12

Add the doubles.

5. 4 + 4 = _____

6. 7 + 7 = _____

7. 9 + 9 = _____

8. 5 + 5 = _____

Solve the word problems. Show your work.

9. | Leah has 12 beads. She needs 7 more beads to finish a necklace.

How many beads in all does she need to make her necklace?

_____ + _____ = _____ **beads**

10. | Brett had 8 cards in one pile and 6 cards in another pile.

How many cards will he have if he makes one pile of cards?

_____ + _____ = _____ **cards**

| Started: | Finished: | Total Time: | Completed: | Correct: |

Addition Sums to 20

Name _____   Date _____

Fill in the boxes for each addition problem.

1. $4 + $ _____ $= 10$

2. _____ $+ 5 = 10$

3. $3 + $ _____ $= 10$

4. _____ $+ 8 = 10$

Solve the word problems. Show your work.

5. Shelley has four soccer balls and five beach balls. How many balls does she have altogether?

_____ $+$ _____ $=$ _____ **balls**

6. Colton read his book for six hours the first week. He read for four hours the second week.

In all, how many hours did he read his book?

_____ $+$ _____ $=$ _____ **hours**

Solve the addition problems.

7. $\begin{array}{r} 4 \\ + 6 \\ \hline \end{array}$

8. $\begin{array}{r} 9 \\ + 5 \\ \hline \end{array}$

9. $\begin{array}{r} 7 \\ + 7 \\ \hline \end{array}$

10. $\begin{array}{r} 5 \\ + 4 \\ \hline \end{array}$

Started:	Finished:	Total Time:	Completed:	Correct:

Addition Sums to 20

Name _____ Date _____

Fill in the boxes for each addition problem.

1. _____ + 5 = 15

2. 11 + 5 = _____

3. 7 + _____ = 14

4. 12 + _____ = 20

Find the sums.

5.   8
    + 5
      ____

6.   6
    + 8
      ____

7.   8
    + 7
      ____

Add the doubles.

8. 6 + 6 = _____

9. 8 + 8 = _____

Solve the word problem. Show your work.

10.	Emma had 10 dolls and Ella had 4 dolls. Together, how many dolls do they have?

_____ + _____ = _____ **dolls**

Name _____   Date _____

Find the sums.

| 1. | 9
+ 9 | 2. | 6
+ 9 | 3. | 9
+ 8 | 4. | 10
+ 10 |

Use four different sets of factors to equal 15.

5. _____ + _____ = 15

6. _____ + _____ = 15

7. _____ + _____ = 15

8. _____ + _____ = 15

Solve the word problems. Show your work.

9. | Gigi had nine blocks and her brother had 11 blocks. They used all the blocks to build a tower. How many blocks did they use?

+ _____

blocks

10. | George loves cookies. He ate 13 cookies on the weekend and six more on Tuesday! How many cookies did George eat?

+ _____

cookies

| Started: | Finished: | Total Time: | Completed: | Correct: |

Name _____ Date _____

Add three numbers to find the sums.

1.	6	2.	7	3.	9
	6		3		7
	+ 3		+ 4		+ 1

Find the missing factor for each addition problem.

4. $2 + 8 +$ _____ $= 17$

5. _____ $+ 4 + 6 = 19$

6. $5 +$ _____ $+ 6 = 16$

7. _____ $+ 3 + 7 = 18$

Use the numbers in the boxes to make addition problems.

8. | 7   16   9 |

_____ + _____ = _____

9. | 13   10   3 |

_____ + _____ = _____

10. | 9   13   4 |

_____ + _____ = _____

Started:	Finished:	Total Time:	Completed:	Correct:

2-Digit Addition

Name _____ Date _____

Find the sums.

1.   12
      + 12

2.   42
      + 53

3.   21
      + 28

4.   36
      + 41

Solve the problems.

5. 77 + 10 = _____

6. 60 + 20 = _____

7. 55 + 5 = _____

8. 90 + 10 = _____

Solve the word problems. Show your work.

9. Bob has 50 chickens in his coop. He added 17 more. How many chickens are in the coop now?

+ _____

chickens

10. Cara likes to watch the ducks at the park. On Tuesday she counted 23 ducks. On Thursday she saw 54 ducks! How many ducks did she see altogether?

+ _____

ducks

Started:	Finished:	Total Time:	Completed:	Correct:

Name _____   Date _____

Circle the *odd* numbers.

1.   23   44   65   16   11

2.   38   59   40   13   21

Circle the *even* numbers.

3.   42   33   76   15   24

4.   86   55   62   34   17

Find the sums.

5.   24   6.   21   7.   70
      + 32   + 18   + 16

Find the missing factor for the addition problem.

8. 50 + 40 + _____ = 95

Solve the word problems. Show your work.

9.	Jaycee won 28 tickets playing pinball and 51 tickets on the video game. How many tickets did she have in total?

                                        + _____
                                                tickets

10.	Zeke counted 35 scissors in the classroom and he counted another 62 scissors in the storeroom. How many scissors did he count?

                                        + _____
                                                scissors

Started:	Finished:	Total Time:	Completed:	Correct:

2-Digit Addition

Name _____   Date _____

Find the sums of two numbers.

1.	47	2.	60	3.	53	4.	70
	+ 31		+ 14		+ 35		+ 29

Find the sums of three numbers.

5.	22	6.	12	7.	60
	33		33		23
	+ 44		+ 42		+ 15

Find the missing factor for each addition problem.

8. 25 + 25 + _____ = 100   **9.** 30 + _____ + 30 = 80

Solve the word problem. Show your work.

10. Mr. Jones used 42 tacks to put up his Math bulletin board, 36 tacks for his Reading bulletin board, and 11 tacks for his Science board. How many tacks did he use for all three boards?

+ _____

tacks

Started:	Finished:	Total Time:	Completed:	Correct:

Name _____   Date _____

Find the sums.

1.	614	2.	342	3.	523	4.	611
	+ 255		+ 517		+ 441		+ 318

Solve the problems.

5. 345 + 100 = _____

6. 762 + 200 = _____

7. 595 + 300 = _____

8. 892 + 100 = _____

Solve the word problems. Show your work.

9. The class collected 125 pencils in January and 342 pencils in February. How many pencils did they collect in two months?

 +_____

pencils

10. Mrs. Jonas has 200 red crayons and 175 blue crayons. How many crayons does she have?

+_____

crayons

Started:	Finished:	Total Time:	Completed:	Correct:

Name _____ Date _____

Solve the problems.

1. 161 + 500 = _____

2. 395 + 400 = _____

3. 478 + 300 = _____

4. 231 + 200 = _____

Find the sums.

5.   159
     + 630

6.   545
     + 342

7.   816
     + 123

8.   143
     + 636

Solve the word problems. Show your work.

9. There are 251 students in Julian's school and 327 students in the school around the corner. How many students are in both schools?

+ _____

students

10. At Back-to-School night, 425 parents came to see the first grade classes and 432 parents came to see the second grade classes.
How many parents came to see the classes?

+ _____

parents

Started:	Finished:	Total Time:	Completed:	Correct:

Name _____   Date _____

Regroup and add to find the sums.

1.   11
  + 89
	2. 18
	  + 23
		3. 62
		  + 9
			4. 37
			  + 27

Find the sums of three numbers.

5.   24
    33
  + 24
	6. 35
	    21
	  + 36
		7. 14
		    70
		  + 16

Solve the word problems. Show your work.

8. | Tilly made 36 cupcakes for the Bake Sale. Uri made 48 cupcakes.
How many cupcakes did Tilly and Uri bring to the Bake Sale?

+ _____

9. | Kai's family went to a farm to pick apples. Kai picked 25 apples, his dad
picked 34 apples, and his sister picked 21 apples.
How many apples did they pick altogether?

+ _____

10. | In the bike rack at school, Scott counted 36 red bikes and 34 black bikes.
How many bikes did Scott count altogether?

+ _____

Started:	Finished:	Total Time:	Completed:	Correct:

Name _____ Date _____

Use the information below to answer each question. Regroup and add.

The second graders had a jumping contest.
They recorded their best jumps.

Casey	59 inches
Luke	85 inches
Heather	61 inches
Mary	86 inches
James	85 inches
Leni	60 inches

1. How far did Luke and Leni jump?

+ _____

2. How far did Casey and Mary jump?

+ _____

3. How far did Mary and James jump?

+ _____

4. How far did James and Leni jump?

+ _____

5. How far did Heather and Casey jump?

+ _____

6. How far did Luke and Heather jump?

+ _____

7. How far did Casey and James jump? _____

8. Who jumped the *longest* distance? _____

9. Who jumped the *shortest* distance? _____

10. Which two jumpers jumped the same distance?

_____   _____

Started:	Finished:	Total Time:	Completed:	Correct:

Name _____   Date _____

Answer the questions about the number in the oval on the right.

   1. Which number is in the *ones* place? _____

   2. How many *hundreds* are there? _____   (**958**)

   3. Which number is in the *tens* place? _____

Regroup and add to find the sums.

   4.   134
       + 276

   5.   435
       + 284

   6.   741
       + 249

   7.   617
       + 207

   8.   349
       + 231

Solve the word problems. Show your work.

9. There were 127 people on the first plane, and 184 people travelled on the second plane. How many people travelled on both planes?

   + _____
        people

10. Peyton read 495 pages during her vacation and Aria read 232 pages. How many pages did they read altogether?

   + _____
        pages

Started:	Finished:	Total Time:	Completed:	Correct:

Name _____   Date _____

Solve the word problems. Show your work.

1. Erica has two new boxes of crayons. Each box of crayons has 96 crayons. How many crayons does she have?

+ _____

crayons

2. There are 365 days in a year. How many days are there in two years?

+ _____

days

Solve.

3. What is 200 plus 600? _____

4. What is 300 plus 400? _____

Regroup and add to find the sums.

5. 245 + 386	6. 863 + 47	7. 349 + 231
8. 439 + 242	9. 856 + 137	10. 198 + 196

Started:	Finished:	Total Time:	Completed:	Correct:

Name _____   Date _____

Regroup and add to find the sums.

1.   649
   + 141

2.   88
   + 22

3.   753
   + 98

4.   652
   + 179

5.   495
   + 335

6.   80
   + 120

Find the totals. Try to add in your head.

7. $50 + 150 = $ _____

8. $250 + 100 + 50 = $ _____

More adding and regrouping!

9.   277
   + 39

10.   254
   + 216

Started:	Finished:	Total Time:	Completed:	Correct:

Name _____   Date _____

Count by 2s. Fill in the missing numbers.

1. 2, _____, 6, _____, 10

2. 6, _____, 10, 12, _____

3. 4, _____, _____, 10, 12

Count by 2s. Write the total number of items on the line.

4.    _____ boots

5.    _____ mittens

6.      _____ cupcakes

Write each addition problem as a multiplication problem.

7. 2 + 2 + 2 + 2 + 2 = _____   _____ × _____ = _____

8. 2 + 2 + 2 + 2 + 2 + 2 + 2 = _____   _____ × _____ = _____

9. 2 + 2 + 2 + 2 + 2 + 2 + 2 + 2 + 2 = _____   _____ × _____ = _____

10. 2 + 2 + 2 + 2 + 2 + 2 + 2 + 2 = _____   _____ × _____ = _____

Started:	Finished:	Total Time:	Completed:	Correct:

Name _____   Date _____

Count by 3s. Fill in the missing numbers.

1. 3, _____, 9, _____, 15

2. 6, _____, 12, _____, 18

3. 9, _____, 15, _____, 21

Count by 3s. Write the total number of items on the line.

4.   _____ **buttons**

5.   _____ **blueberries**

6.   _____ **stars**

Write each addition problem as a multiplication problem.

7. 3 + 3 + 3 + 3 = _____   _____ × _____ = _____

8. 3 + 3 + 3 + 3 + 3 = _____   _____ × _____ = _____

9. 3 + 3 + 3 + 3 + 3 + 3 = _____   _____ × _____ = _____

10. 3 + 3 + 3 + 3 + 3 + 3 + 3 = _____   _____ × _____ = _____

| Started: | Finished: | Total Time: | Completed: | Correct: |

Name _____ Date _____

Count by 5s. Fill in the missing numbers.

1. 5, 10, _____, 20, _____

2. 10, _____ , _____, 25, 30

3. 15, _____, 25, _____, 35

Count by 5s. Write the total number of items on the line.

4.   _____ puppies

5.     _____ hot dogs

6.    _____ frogs

Write each addition problem as a multiplication problem.

7. 5 + 5 + 5 + 5 + 5 + 5 = _____   _____ × _____ = _____

8. 5 + 5 + 5 + 5 + 5 + 5 + 5 + 5 + 5 = _____   _____ × _____ = _____

9. 5 + 5 + 5 + 5 + 5 + 5 + 5 = _____   _____ × _____ = _____

10. 5 + 5 + 5 + 5 + 5 + 5 + 5 + 5 + 5 + 5 = _____   _____ × _____ = _____

Started:	Finished:	Total Time:	Completed:	Correct:

Name _____ Date _____

Count by 10s. Fill in the missing numbers.

1. 10, _____, 30, _____

2. 30, _____, _____, 60

3. 40, _____, 60, _____, 80

4. 50, 60, _____, 80,_____

Each domino has 10 dots on it. How many dots are there in each group?

5. 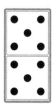 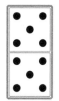 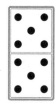   _____ dots

6. 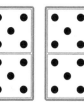   _____ dots

Write each addition problem as a multiplication problem.

7. 10 + 10 + 10 + 10 + 10 + 10 = _____

_____ × _____ = _____

8. 10 + 10 + 10 + 10 + 10 + 10 + 10 + 10 = _____

_____ × _____ = _____

9. 10 + 10 + 10 + 10 + 10 + 10 + 10 = _____

_____ × _____ = _____

10. 10 + 10 + 10 + 10 + 10 + 10 + 10 + 10 + 10 + 10 = _____

_____ × _____ = _____

Started:	Finished:	Total Time:	Completed:	Correct:

Name _____   Date _____

Write an addition problem and a multiplication problem for each group of cherries.

1. Addition: _____

2. Multiplication: _____

3. Addition: _____

4. Multiplication: _____

5. Addition: _____

6. Multiplication: _____

7. Addition: _____

8. Multiplication: _____

9. Addition: _____

10. Multiplication: _____

Started:	Finished:	Total Time:	Completed:	Correct:

Name _____ Date _____

Write an addition problem and a multiplication problem for each group of happy faces.

1. Addition: _____

2. Multiplication: _____

3. Addition: _____

4. Multiplication: _____

5. Addition: _____

6. Multiplication: _____

7. Addition: _____

8. Multiplication: _____

9. Addition: _____

10. Multiplication: _____

Started:	Finished:	Total Time:	Completed:	Correct:

Name _____ Date _____

Find the differences.

1. $10 - 7 =$ _____

2. $12 - 5 =$ _____

3. $9 - 6 =$ _____

4. $11 - 4 =$ _____

Find the missing number for each subtraction problem.

5. $12 -$ _____ $= 6$

6. _____ $- 7 = 6$

7. $15 -$ _____ $= 9$

8. _____ $- 4 = 10$

Use the number in the box to make a subtraction problem.

9.

| 7 | 12 | 5 |

_____ – _____ = _____

Solve the word problem. Show your work.

| **10.** | Jace has 18 shirts. Nine shirts are red and the rest are blue. How many shirts are blue? |

_____ – _____ = _____ shirts

| Started: | Finished: | Total Time: | Completed: | Correct: |

2-Digit Subtraction

Name _____ Date _____

Find the missing number for each subtraction problem.

1. 19 – _____ = 10

2. _____ – 6 = 6

3. 20 – _____ = 15

4. _____ – 8 = 8

Find the differences.

5. 15 – 7 = _____

6. 9 – 5 = _____

7. 18 – 9 = _____

Use the numbers in the boxes to make subtraction problems.

8.

| 8 | 17 | 9 |

_____ – _____ = _____

9.

| 4 | 11 | 7 |

_____ – _____ = _____

Solve the word problem. Show your work.

10. Simone had 15 books. She put nine books on her shelf and took the rest to school. How many books did Simone take to school?

_____ **books**

Name _____   Date _____

Find the differences.

1. $13 - 6 =$ _____

2. $15 - 8 =$ _____

3. $9 - 4 =$ _____

4. $16 - 7 =$ _____

Find the missing factor for each subtraction problem.

5.   14
          − 7
          ‾‾‾

6.   18
          − 9
          ‾‾‾

7.   16
          − 8
          ‾‾‾

8.   20
          − 10
          ‾‾‾

Use the numbers in the boxes to make a subtraction problem.

9.

| 7 | 16 | 9 |

_____ − _____ = _____

10.

| 6 | 14 | 8 |

_____ − _____ = _____

| Started: | Finished: | Total Time: | Completed: | Correct: |

Name _____ Date _____

Solve the problems.

1. 34
    − 23

2. 56
    − 43

3. 88
    − 76

Find the differences.

4. 90 − 10 = _____

5. 70 − 30 = _____

6. 40 − 20 = _____

Solve each subtraction problem.

7. 63
    − 42

8. 28
    − 15

9. 63
    − 42

Solve the word problem. Show your work.

| 10. | Talia has two dogs. Whopper weighs 89 pounds. Teacup weighs 16 pounds. |

How much more does Whopper weigh?

− _____

pounds

| Started: | Finished: | Total Time: | Completed: | Correct: |

Name _____ Date _____

Solve each subtraction problem.

1.	88 − 57	**2.**	67 − 35	**3.**	75 − 31	**4.**	59 − 47

Solve the word problems. Show your work.

5. The skateboard costs $87, and the scooter costs $53. How much more money does the skateboard cost than the scooter?

− _____

6. Tal's brother is saving up to buy a bike that costs $99. He has saved $48 so far. How much more money does he need?

− _____

Find the differences.

7.	69 − 42		**8.**	55 − 34
9.	76 − 22		**10.**	93 − 50

Started:	Finished:	Total Time:	Completed:	Correct:

Name _____   Date _____

Solve each subtraction problem.

1. $\begin{array}{r} 234 \\ -\ 123 \\ \hline \end{array}$

2. $\begin{array}{r} 679 \\ -\ 549 \\ \hline \end{array}$

3. $\begin{array}{r} 847 \\ -\ 325 \\ \hline \end{array}$

4. $\begin{array}{r} 589 \\ -\ 457 \\ \hline \end{array}$

5. $\begin{array}{r} 965 \\ -\ 564 \\ \hline \end{array}$

6. $\begin{array}{r} 799 \\ -\ 786 \\ \hline \end{array}$

Find the differences.

7. $800 - 500 =$ _____

8. $500 - 300 =$ _____

9. $300 - 200 =$ _____

Solve the word problem. Show your work.

10. The class memory book has 244 pages. They have completed 122 pages.

    How many more pages do they have to complete?

    $-$ _____

    pages

Started:	Finished:	Total Time:	Completed:	Correct:

Name _____   Date _____

Find the differences.

| 1. | 854
− 731 | 2. | 948
− 524 | 3. | 556
− 532 | 4. | 629
− 318 |

Try solving these subtraction problems in your head.

5. $980 - 50 =$ _____

6. $450 - 30 =$ _____

7. $720 - 20 =$ _____

8. $350 - 40 =$ _____

Solve the word problems. Show your work.

| 9. | Tad had 458 trading cards. He lost 237 cards. How many cards does he have left? |

−_____

cards

| 10. | Billy had 600 trading cards. He gave 200 cards to his friend Tad. How many cards does Billy have now? |

−_____

cards

| Started: | Finished: | Total Time: | Completed: | Correct: |

Name _____ Date _____

Try solving these subtraction problems in your head.

1. 160 – 40 = _____

2. 390 – 50 = _____

3. 560 – 30 = _____

4. 240 – 40 = _____

Find the differences.

5. 762
   – 631

6. 456
   – 354

7. 995
   – 860

8. 178
   – 65

Fill in the blanks to solve the problems.

9. 7 7 8
   – 3 __ 8
   _____
    4 5 0

10. 9 8 8
    – 4 5 __
    _____
     5 3 5

Name _____   Date _____

Regroup and subtract these 2-digit numbers.

1. 70	2. 42	3. 56	4. 64	5. 32
− 25	− 33	− 18	− 58	− 18

Try solving these subtraction problems in your head.

6. 50 − 25 = _____

7. 100 − 20 = _____

8. 20 − 8 = _____

Solve the word problems. Show your work.

9. Diem had 25 bracelets. She gave 16 to her sister.
How many bracelets does she have left?

= _____

bracelets

10. Sal had 24 crayons. She used 16 for a science project. How many crayons does she have left?

= _____

crayons

Started:	Finished:	Total Time:	Completed:	Correct:

Name _____   Date _____

Regroup and subtract these 2-digit numbers.

1. 77
   − 59

2. 21
   − 12

3. 34
   − 16

4. 56
   − 37

Regroup and subtract these 3-digit numbers.

5. 462
   − 309

6. 598
   − 509

7. 342
   − 282

8. 700
   − 633

Solve the problems.

9. 52
   − 38

10. 603
    − 505

Started:	Finished:	Total Time:	Completed:	Correct:

Name _____   Date _____

Regroup and subtract these 3-digit numbers.

1.   661
     − 562

2.   816
     − 372

3.   269
     − 89

4.   429
     − 275

Fill in the blanks to solve the problems.

5.   3 8 6
     − 2 __ 7
     ‾‾‾‾‾‾
     1 4 9

6.   6 7 __
     − 5 9 1
     ‾‾‾‾‾‾
       8 5

Try solving these subtraction problems in your head.

7. 100 − 25 = _____

8. 100 − 50 = _____

9. 100 − 75 = _____

10. 300 − 250 = _____

Started:	Finished:	Total Time:	Completed:	Correct:

Name _____ Date _____

Solve the problems for the fact family.

1.　　6
　　+ 7
　　―――

2.　　7
　　+ 6
　　―――

3.　　13
　　− 7
　　―――

4.　　13
　　− 6
　　―――

Use the correct sign (+ or −) for each set of numbers.

5. 15 ◯ 6 = 9

6. 8 ◯ 6 = 14

7. 19 ◯ 10 = 9

8. 5 ◯ 6 = 11

Solve the problems.

9.　　53
　　+ 41
　　―――

10.　　58
　　− 25
　　―――

Started:	Finished:	Total Time:	Completed:	Correct:

Mixed Equations

Name _____   Date _____

Solve the problems.

1.	23	2.	243	3.	98	4.	765
	+ 43		+ 543		− 67		− 632

Use the correct sign (+ or −) for each set of numbers.

5. 25 ⬭ 5 = 30

6. 18 ⬭ 9 = 9

7. 50 ⬭ 25 = 75

8. 22 ⬭ 10 = 32

Solve the word problems. Show your work.

9.	There are three fourth grade classes at Tia's school. Each class has 20 students. How many students are there altogether?
	_____ students

10.	Lee has 45 toys on the shelves in his room. He decided to give 15 to his brother. How many toys does he have left?
	_____ toys

Name _____   Date _____

Use the correct sign (+ or –) for each set of numbers.

1. 8 $\bigcirc$ 8 = 16   2. 22 $\bigcirc$ 11 = 11

3. 50 $\bigcirc$ 25 = 25   4. 18 $\bigcirc$ 2 = 20

Regroup and solve the problems.

5.   73
    – 56

6.   53
    + 23

7.   100
      75
    + 25

8.   85
    – 68

Solve the word problems. Show your work.

9.	Cody had 230 bikes for sale in his store. He sold 45 bikes over the weekend.

How many bikes are in the store after his sales?

_____ **bikes**

10.	Bonnie had 83 swimmers on her swim team but 17 left. How many swimmers does she have now?

_____ **swimmers**

Started:	Finished:	Total Time:	Completed:	Correct:

Name _____   Date _____

Regroup and solve the addition problems.

1.   678
    + 132

2.   244
    + 656

3.   278
    + 552

4.   453
    + 307

Regroup and solve the subtraction problems.

5.   66
    − 48

6.   742
    − 543

7.   85
    − 36

8.   344
    − 236

Rewrite and solve the problems.

9. one hundred minus fifty-three equals _____

10. three hundred twenty-four plus two hundred fifty-nine equals _____

Started:	Finished:	Total Time:	Completed:	Correct:

Name _____ Date _____

Circle the correct answer to measure the length of each object.

1. What would you use to measure the length of a football field?

    A. inches   **B.** yards   **C.** miles

2. Which measurement would you use to measure the length of a car?

    A. inches   **B.** feet   **C.** miles

3. Which measurement would you use to measure the length of a shoe?

    A. inches   **B.** yards   **C.** miles

4. Which measurement would you use to measure the length of a pencil?

    A. inches   **B.** yards   **C.** miles

Find each measurement.

5. How many inches long is the toy truck?

_____ **inches**

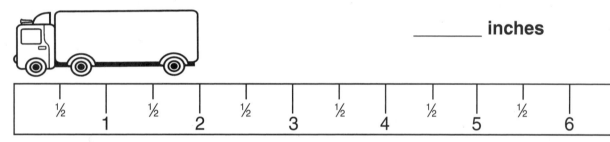

6. How many inches long is the pencil?

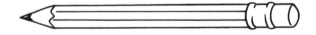

_____ **inches**

Answer *True* or *False* to each statement.

7. A baby shoe is about one foot long.   **True**   **False**

8. A car is longer than a bathtub.   **True**   **False**

9. A lunchbox is about two feet long.   **True**   **False**

10. A bumblebee is about one inch long.   **True**   **False**

Started:	Finished:	Total Time:	Completed:	Correct:

Name _____ Date _____

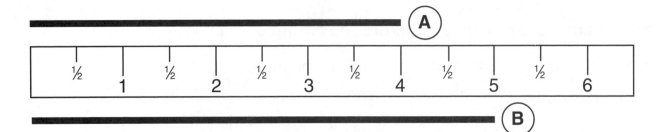

1. How long is the line above the ruler? _____ **inches**

2. How long is the line below the ruler? _____ **inches**

3. Which line above is shorter? Circle your answer. Ⓐ Ⓑ

Use the chart to answer questions 4–10.

frog	rabbit	horse	kangaroo
3'	4'	8'	9'

4. How far did the rabbit jump? _____

5. How far did the frog jump? _____

6. How far did the kangaroo jump? _____

7. How far did the horse jump? _____

8. Which animal jumped the shortest distance? _____

9. Which animal jumped the longest distance? _____

10. How much farther did the rabbit jump than the frog?

_____ – _____ = _____

Started:	Finished:	Total Time:	Completed:	Correct:

Name _____   Date _____

Look at the distance each car traveled each day. Answer questions 1–7.

Monday	10 miles
Tuesday	40 miles
Wednesday	30 miles
Thursday	20 miles
Friday	40 miles

1. How far did the car travel on Wednesday? _____ **miles**

2. How far did the car travel on Monday and Tuesday?

   _____ + _____ + _____ = _____ **miles**

3. On which day did the car travel the shortest distance? _____

4. On which two days did the car travel the same distance?

   _____   _____

5. How far did the car travel on Thursday and Friday?

   _____ + _____ + _____ = _____ **miles**

6. How far did the car travel on the first three days?

   _____ + _____ + _____ = _____ **miles**

7. How far did the car travel on Tuesday and Friday? _____ + _____ = _____

Solve the problems.

| 8. | 48 | 9. | 39 | 10. | 35 |
| | + 30 | | + 18 | | + 35 |

| Started: | Finished: | Total Time: | Completed: | Correct: |

Name _____ Date _____

Find each measurement.

1. How many centimeters long is the pencil? _____ **cm**

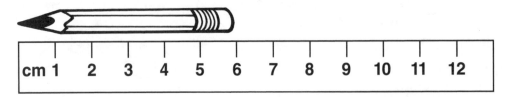

2. How many centimeters long would two 5 cm pencils be? _____ **cm**

3. How many centimeters long is the rectangle?

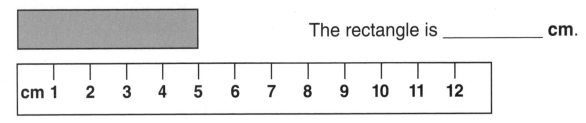

The rectangle is _____ **cm**.

4. How long would two 8 cm rectangles be? _____ **cm**

What would you use to measure each item? Circle your answers.

5. length of a swimming pool   **centimeters**   **meters**

6. length of a paintbrush   **centimeters**   **meters**

7. length of a school bus   **centimeters**   **meters**

8. length of a grasshopper   **centimeters**   **meters**

How long is each piece of ribbon in centimeters?

9. _____ **centimeters**

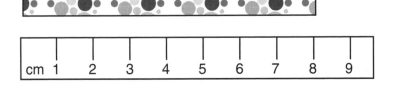

10. _____ **centimeters**

Started:	Finished:	Total Time:	Completed:	Correct:

Name _____   Date _____

Use the metric rulers to find the length of each line.

1. Line 1 is _____ cm long.

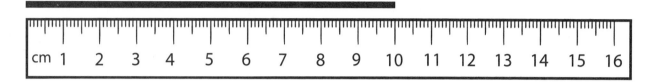

2. Line 2 is _____ cm long.

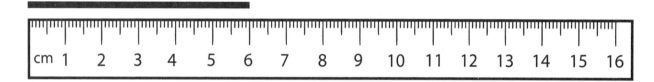

3. Line 3 is _____ cm long.

4. Line 4 is _____ cm long.

Add to solve.	**Subtract to solve.**
5. 7 cm + 3 cm = _____	**8.** 14 cm – 6 cm = _____
6. 6 cm + 5 cm = _____	**9.** 6 cm – 3 cm = _____
7. 7 cm + 7 cm = _____	**10.** 12 cm – 7 cm = _____

Started:	Finished:	Total Time:	Completed:	Correct:

Name _____   Date _____

Use the trees at the right to answer the questions.

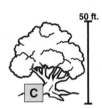

1. Which tree is the tallest? _____

2. Which tree is the shortest? _____

3. Add the height of Tree **A** and Tree **B**.

   _____ + _____ = _____

4. Add the height of Tree **A**, Tree **B**, and Tree **C**. What is the total?

   _____ + _____ + _____ = _____

5. What is the difference in height between Tree **B** and Tree **C**?

   _____ − _____ = _____

6. What is the difference in height between Tree **B** and Tree **A**?

   _____ − _____ = _____

Answer the questions below about height. Circle your answers.

7. Which is taller, a duck or a horse?   **duck**   **horse**

8. Which is taller, a motorcycle or a bus?   **motorcycle**   **bus**

9. Which is shorter, an inch or a foot?   **inch**   **foot**

Solve the word problem. Show your work.

10.	Carlos built a tower that was 18 inches tall. Jay's tower was 14 inches taller.

                                      +_____

How tall was Jay's tower? _____ **inches**

Started:	Finished:	Total Time:	Completed:	Correct:

Name _____ Date _____

Circle the correct letter for the answer to each question.

1. Which pencil is the tallest?

A   **B**   **C**   **D**

2. Which pencil is the shortest?

A   **B**   **C**   **D**

3. Which two pencils are the same size?

A   **B**   **C**   **D**

Answer *True* or *False*.

4. 12 inches = 1 foot	**True**	**False**
5. 4 inches + 4 inches + 4 inches = 1 foot	**True**	**False**
6. 4 inches + 6 inches = 1 foot	**True**	**False**
7. 6 inches + 6 inches = 1 foot	**True**	**False**

Solve the word problems.

8.	Aiden is six feet tall and Grace is four feet tall. How much taller is Aiden? _____ **feet taller**
9.	Jack's ladder is 12 feet tall. Mr. Green's ladder is seven feet tall. How much taller is Jack's ladder? _____ **feet taller**
10.	Susan's wall was 12 inches tall. Then she added six more inches of blocks. How tall was the wall after she added six inches? _____ **inches**

Started:	Finished:	Total Time:	Completed:	Correct:

Name _____   Date _____

Answer *True* or *False* for each statement.

1. 6 inches + 6 inches = 1 foot   **True**   **False**

2. 13 inches < 1 foot   **True**   **False**

3. 4 inches + 4 inches + 4 inches = 1 foot   **True**   **False**

Fill in the blank to complete each problem.

4. _____ inches + 8 inches = one foot

5. 5 inches + _____ inches = one foot

6. _____ inches + 9 inches = one foot

> **12 inches = 1 foot**

Answer the questions about the backpacks.

A	B	C
12 pounds	**5 pounds**	**8 pounds**

7. Which backpack is the heaviest?   **A**   **B**   **C**

8. Which backpack weighs the least?   **A**   **B**   **C**

9. How much do backpack **B** and backpack **C** weigh together? _____

10. How much more does backpack **A** weigh than backpack **C**? _____

Started:	Finished:	Total Time:	Completed:	Correct:

Name _____ Date _____

Use the weight chart to answer *Yes* or *No* to the questions.

There are 5 piles of newspapers to move. The wagon can carry 23 pounds.

Pile 1	25 pounds
Pile 2	15 pounds
Pile 3	22 pounds
Pile 4	8 pounds
Pile 5	17 pounds

1. Can the wagon carry Pile 1?   **Yes   No**

2. Can the wagon carry Pile 5?   **Yes   No**

3. Can the wagon carry Pile 2 and Pile 4 together?   **Yes   No**

4. Can the wagon carry Pile 4 and Pile 5 together?   **Yes   No**

5. Can the wagon carry Pile 3?   **Yes   No**

Use the chart to solve the problems.

Dog 1	Dog 2	Dog 3	Dog 4
29 pounds	18 pounds	38 pounds	50 pounds

6. How much does the heaviest dog weigh? _____

7. How much does the lightest dog weigh? _____

8. How much do the heaviest and the lightest dogs weigh together? _____

9. How much do Dog 1 and Dog 3 weigh together? _____

10. How much do Dog 3 and Dog 4 weigh together? _____

Started:	Finished:	Total Time:	Completed:	Correct:

Name _____   Date _____

Write the time for each analog clock.

1. _____   2. _____   3. _____   4. _____

Circle the correct time.

5.	6.	7.
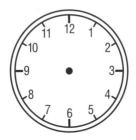		
10:15 11:15 11:03	**1:45 2:45 9:15**	**6:15 4:15 5:15**

Draw hands on the clock to show the time.

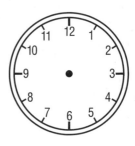

8. 8:45   **9.** 3:15

Answer the question. Circle *True* or *False*.

10. 12:00 a.m. and 12:00 p.m. look the same on an analog clock.

                True   **False**

Started:	Finished:	Total Time:	Completed:	Correct:

Name _____ Date _____

Circle the correct time shown on each digital clock.

1. **2:30**   two thirty   three thirty

2. **12:15**   twelve fifteen   three o'clock

3. **7:30**   six thirty   seven thirty

Fill in each digital clock with the time shown.

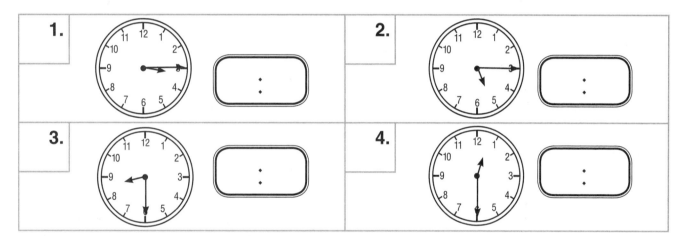

1.

2.

3.

4.

Circle the clock with the correct time.

8. Kaden wakes up at seven twenty. She has breakfast at seven fifty. Which clock shows what time she has breakfast?

   7:20   **7:40**   **7:50**

9. It is 4:00. Joel needs to read for 20 minutes before he can play. What time can Joel go out and play?

   4:40   **3:40**   **4:20**

10. Kailer's bedtime is eight forty-five p.m. Which clock shows his bedtime?

   8:35   **8:45**   **8:40**

| Started: | Finished: | Total Time: | Completed: | Correct: |

Name _____   Date _____

Circle the correct time.

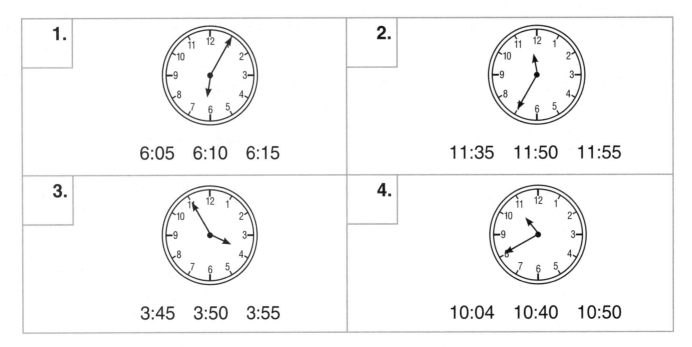

1. 6:05   6:10   6:15

2. 11:35   11:50   11:55

3. 3:45   3:50   3:55

4. 10:04   10:40   10:50

Draw hands on the clock to show the time.

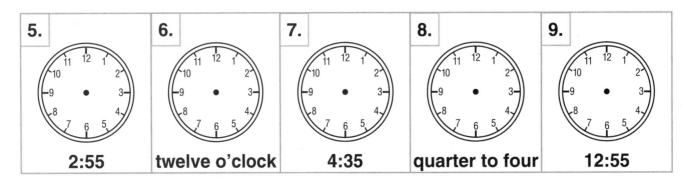

5. 2:55   **6.** twelve o'clock   **7.** 4:35   **8.** quarter to four   **9.** 12:55

Circle the correct answer.

10. Mason started his homework at 12:00 p.m. He did math for 20 minutes and reading for 20 minutes. What time did he finish his homework?

12:40   12:20   12:30

Started:	Finished:	Total Time:	Completed:	Correct:

Name _____ Date _____

Look at each clock. Tell what time it is now, and what time it will be after three hours.

1. Time now: _____

    Time in three hours: _____

2. Time now: _____

    Time in three hours: _____

3. Time now: _____

    Time in three hours: _____

What time will it be in a half hour?

4. Time now: | 1:30 | Time in half hour: _____

5. Time now: | 9:15 | Time in half hour: _____

6. Time now: | 7:45 | Time in half hour: _____

Draw hands on the analog clocks to show the time.

7. quarter after nine 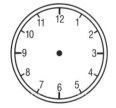   8. four fifty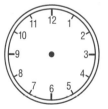

Show the times on the digital clocks.

9. six twenty-five    10. nine forty-five [:   ]

| Started: | Finished: | Total Time: | Completed: | Correct: |

Name _____   Date _____

Answer the questions. Show your work.

1. Cole's practice started at 6 p.m. Practice was for one hour. What time did practice end?

Start Time:  **End Time:** _____

2. Linsi wanted to practice skating for 20 minutes. She started at 3:10 p.m. What time did she finish? Show the time on the digital clock.

Answer *True* or *False* to each statement.

3. Three fifteen and quarter after three are the same time.   **True   False**

4. Half past six and seven thirty are the same time.   **True   False**

5. Five ten and 5:10 are the same time.   **True   False**

6. Noon and midnight look the same on an analog clock.   **True   False**

Use the analog clock on the right to answer questions 7–10 on the digital clocks.

7. Show the time that is on the analog clock.

8. What time will it be in five minutes?

9. What time will it be in fifty minutes?

10. What time will it be in ten minutes?

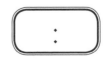

Started:	Finished:	Total Time:	Completed:	Correct:

Name _____ Date _____

Use the clocks to answer the questions. Write the correct letter on the line.

A.  **B.** 9:20 **C.**  **D.** 8:45

1. Which clock shows **twelve twenty**? _____

2. Which clock shows **three forty**? _____

3. Which clock shows **twenty after nine**? _____

4. Which clock shows **eight forty-five**? _____

Show each time on the clock.

5. two forty

6. eleven fifty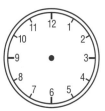

7. seven fifty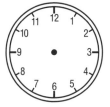

8. twelve ten

Read the word problems and answer the questions.

9.	Kari played soccer for forty minutes. She started at 5 p.m. Write the time she finished in the digital clock. 
10.	Liza ran for one hour at practice. Write what time she finished. **Liza's Start Time:**  **Ending Time:** _____

Started:	Finished:	Total Time:	Completed:	Correct:

Name _____   Date _____

Circle the name of each coin.

1.   penny   nickel   dime   quarter

2.   penny   nickel   dime   quarter

3.   penny   nickel   dime   quarter

4.   penny   nickel   dime   quarter

How much is each coin worth? Circle your answers.

5.   1¢   5¢   10¢   25¢

6.   1¢   5¢   10¢   25¢

7.   1¢   5¢   10¢   25¢

8.   1¢   5¢   10¢   25¢

Answer the questions. Circle the correct number of coins.

9. How many pennies equal one nickel? _____

10. How many pennies equal one dime? _____

Started:	Finished:	Total Time:	Completed:	Correct:

Name _____   Date _____

Answer the questions about coins.

1. How many pennies equal one quarter? _____

2. How many nickels equal one dime? _____

3. How many nickels equal one quarter? _____

Answer the questions about a dollar bill.

4. A dollar bill is the same as _____ pennies.

5. A dollar bill is the same as _____ nickels.

6. A dollar bill is the same as _____ dimes.

7. A dollar bill is the same as _____ quarters.

How much money is in each group?

8. 🪙 + 🪙 + 🪙 = _____¢

9. 🪙 + 🪙 + 🪙 + 🪙 + 🪙 + 🪙 = _____¢

10. 🪙 + 🪙 + 🪙 + 🪙 = _____¢

Started:	Finished:	Total Time:	Completed:	Correct:

Name _____   Date _____

How much money is in each group of quarters? Use the $ or ¢ sign.

1. + + = _____

2. ⬤ + ⬤ + ⬤ + ⬤ = _____

3. ⬤ + ⬤ = _____

4. ⬤ + ⬤ + ⬤ + ⬤ + ⬤ + ⬤ = _____

How much money is in each group of dimes?

5. ⬤ + ⬤ + ⬤ = _____

6. ⬤ + ⬤ + ⬤ + ⬤ + ⬤ + ⬤ = _____

7. ⬤ + ⬤ + ⬤ + ⬤ + ⬤ + ⬤ + ⬤ + ⬤ + ⬤ = _____

How much money is in each group of coins.

8. ⬤ + ⬤ + ⬤ + ⬤ = _____

9. ⬤ + ⬤ + ⬤ + ⬤ + ⬤ = _____

10. ⬤ + ⬤ + ⬤ + ⬤ + ⬤ + ⬤ = _____

Started:	Finished:	Total Time:	Completed:	Correct:

Name _____   Date _____

How much money is in each group of dollar bills?

1. [bill] + [bill] + [bill] = $ _____

2. [bill] + [bill] + [bill] + [bill] + [bill] + [bill] = $ _____

3. [bill] + [bill] + [bill] + [bill] = $ _____

Fill in the blanks to equal each amount.

4. _____ dimes + _____ pennies = 25¢

5. _____ nickels + _____ pennies = 18¢

6. _____ quarters + _____ dimes + _____ pennies = 72¢

Circle the correct amount for each group of money shown.

7. [bill] + [bill] + [quarter] + [quarter]		
$3.50	$3.20	$2.50
8. [bill] + [quarter] + [quarter] + [quarter] + [penny] + [penny]		
$1.60	$1.77	$1.62
9. [bill] + [bill] + [bill] + [bill] + [nickel] + [nickel] + [nickel]		
$4.60	$4.74	$4.15
10. [bill] + [bill] + [dime] + [dime]		
$2.02	$2.20	$2.10

Started:	Finished:	Total Time:	Completed:	Correct:

Name _____   Date _____

Answer the questions about money.

1. You have 2 quarters, 1 dime, and 1 nickel.

How many cents do you have? _____ **cents**

2. You have 1 quarter, 4 dimes, 3 nickels, and 19 pennies.

How many cents do you have? _____ **cents**

3. You have 1 dollar bill, 2 quarters, 2 dimes, and 3 nickels.

How many cents do you have? _____ **cents**

How much money is shown in each group?

4. ⃝ + 💵 + ⃝ + ⃝ + ⃝ + ⃝ = _____

5. ⃝ + ⃝ + 💵 + ⃝ = _____

6. ⃝ + ⃝ + ⃝ + ⃝ + ⃝ + ⃝ + ⃝ + ⃝ = _____

Circle the group of coins in each row that is worth more money.

7. ⃝ + ⃝ + ⃝   **or**   ⃝ + ⃝

8. ⃝ + ⃝ + ⃝ + ⃝   **or**   ⃝ + ⃝ + ⃝ + ⃝

9. ⃝ + ⃝ + ⃝ + ⃝ + ⃝   **or**   ⃝ + ⃝ + ⃝

10. ⃝ + ⃝ + ⃝   **or**   ⃝ + ⃝ + ⃝ + ⃝ + ⃝

Started:	Finished:	Total Time:	Completed:	Correct:

Name _____ Date _____

Use the correct sign (>, <, =) between each group of money.

1. $1.00 ⬭ 🪙 + 🪙 + 🪙 + 🪙

2. 🪙 + 🪙 + 🪙 + 🪙 + 🪙 + 🪙 + 🪙 ⬭ 34¢

3. $1.00 ⬭ 🪙 + 🪙 + 🪙 + 🪙 + 🪙 + 🪙 + 🪙 + 🪙

4. 🪙 + 🪙 + 🪙 + 🪙 + 🪙 + 🪙 + 🪙 ⬭ 42¢

Match the money in each group to the correct total in the box.

5. 🪙 + 🪙 + 🪙 + 🪙 + 🪙 + 🪙 _____

6. 🪙 + 🪙 + 🪙 + 🪙 + 🪙 + 🪙 + 🪙 _____

7. 🪙 + 🪙 + 🪙 + 🪙 _____

| 55¢ |
| 50¢ |
| 35¢ |

Cross out the coin in each row you do not need to buy each item.

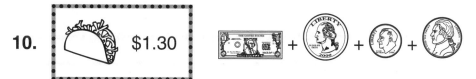

8. 🌭 $1.25   🪙 + 🪙 + 🪙 + 🪙 + 🪙 + 🪙

9. 🍔 $1.55   💵 + 🪙 + 🪙 + 🪙 + 🪙

10. 🌮 $1.30   💵 + 🪙 + 🪙 + 🪙

| Started: | Finished: | Total Time: | Completed: | Correct: |

Name _____ Date _____

Use the picture graph to answer the questions.

Favorite Sport	
Soccer	⚽ ⚽ ⚽ ⚽ ⚽ ⚽ ⚽ ⚽ ⚽ ⚽ ⚽ ⚽
Basketball	🏀 🏀 🏀 🏀 🏀 🏀
Football	🏈 🏈 🏈 🏈 🏈 🏈 🏈

1. Which sport was the favorite? _____

2. Which sport got the least votes? _____

3. How many votes did football get? _____

4. How many votes did soccer get? _____

Count the tally marks to answer the questions.

Slip-ons	👟	IIII IIII
Velcro	👟	IIII III
Laces	👟	IIII IIII

5. What number do these tally marks IIII stand for? _____

6. How many students wore slip-on shoes? _____

7. How many students wore Velcro shoes? _____

8. How many students wore shoes with laces? _____

9. What was the total number of Velcro shoes and slip-ons?

_____ + _____ = _____

10. What was the total number of shoes with laces and slip-ons?

_____ + _____ = _____

Started:	Finished:	Total Time:	Completed:	Correct:

Name _____ Date _____

Four cars were voted on. Answer the questions below.

Car 1	‖‖‖ ‖‖‖ ‖‖
Car 2	‖‖‖ ‖‖‖
Car 3	‖‖‖ ‖‖‖ ‖‖‖ ‖‖‖
Car 4	‖‖‖ ‖‖

1. How many votes did **Car 1** get? _____

2. How many votes did **Car 2** get? _____

3. How many votes did **Car 3** get? _____

4. How many votes did **Car 4** get? _____

5. Which car got the fewest votes?   **Car 1   Car 2   Car 3   Car 4**

6. Which car got the most votes?   **Car 1   Car 2   Car 3   Car 4**

Use the bar graph to answer the questions.

7. Which vehicle got 10 votes?

 car   jet   boat

8. Which vehicle got 15 votes?

 car   jet   boat

9. How many votes did the car get? _____

10. What was the difference between the car votes and the boat votes?

 _____ – _____ = _____

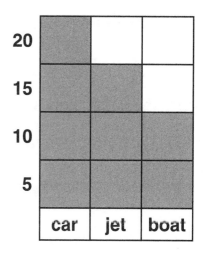

Started:	Finished:	Total Time:	Completed:	Correct:

Name _____   Date _____

Look at the picture graph of favorite fruits. Each fruit stands for 2 votes.

Peach	🍑 🍑 🍑 🍑 🍑
Cherry	🍒 🍒 🍒
Pear	🍐 🍐 🍐 🍐
Banana	🍌 🍌 🍌 🍌 🍌 🍌 🍌

Answer the questions. Remember to count by twos!

1. Which fruit got 10 votes?   **peach   cherry   pear   banana**

2. How many votes did pear get? _____

3. Which fruit got 14 votes?   **peach   cherry   pear   banana**

4. How many votes did cherry get? _____

5. How many more votes did bananas get than peaches?

   _____ – _____ = _____

6. How many votes did cherries and pears get altogether?

   _____ + _____ = _____

Show the tally marks.

7. Show 4 tally marks.

8. Show 10 tally marks.

9. Show 17 tally marks.

10. Show 23 tally marks.

Started:	Finished:	Total Time:	Completed:	Correct:

Name _____ Date _____

Count the tally marks to find the number of each shape.

1. How many ovals? _____

2. How many squares? _____

3. How many triangles? _____

4. How many rectangles? _____

5. How many rhombuses? _____

Ovals	ЖЖ ЖЖ |||
Rectangles	ЖЖ	
Rhombuses	ЖЖ ЖЖ ЖЖ
Squares	ЖЖ |||
Triangles	ЖЖ ЖЖ ||

Do the math and show your work!

6.	Add the squares and the rectangles.
	_____ + _____ = _____

7.	Subtract the rectangles from the triangles.
	_____ + _____ = _____

8.	Add the rectangles and the triangles.
	+ _____

9.	Add the rhombuses and the triangles.
	+ _____

10.	Subtract the squares from the ovals.
	– _____

Started:	Finished:	Total Time:	Completed:	Correct:

Name _____ Date _____

Use the word bank to name the shapes below.

| square   circle   triangle   rhombus   oval   rectangle |

1. _____

2. _____

3. _____

4. _____

5. _____

Answer the questions. Use the word bank above.

6. Name a shape that has three sides. _____

7. Name a shape that has two long sides and two short sides.

_____

8. What is another name for a diamond shape? _____

9. Name a shape that has four equal sides. _____

A quadrilateral has four straight sides.

10. Which shape below is not a quadrilateral? _____

A.   B.   C.   D.

| Started: | Finished: | Total Time: | Completed: | Correct: |

Name _____   Date _____

Use the word bank to name the shapes below.

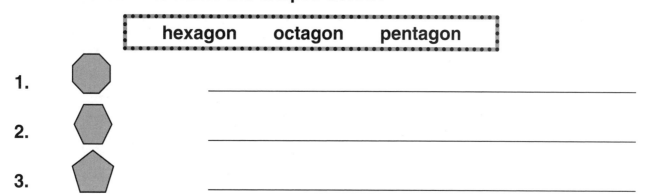

| hexagon | octagon | pentagon |

1. _____

2. _____

3. _____

Answer the questions. Use the word bank above.

4. Name the shape that has six sides. _____

5. Name the shape that has eight sides. _____

6. Name the shape that has five sides. _____

Circle the shape that does not belong in each row.

7.

8.

9.

Circle your answer.

10. Which two shapes could you use to make a rhombus?

2 circles   **2 triangles**   **2 squares**

Started:	Finished:	Total Time:	Completed:	Correct:

Name _____   Date _____

Use the word bank to name the shapes below.

| cube | sphere | cone | prism | cylinder |

1. _____   2. _____   3. _____

4. _____   5. _____

Answer the questions. Use the word bank above.

6. Which shape has two triangle faces and three rectangle faces?

_____

7. Name two shapes that have curved faces.

_____ _____

8. Which shape is like a ball? _____

9. Which shape has a circle face at each end? _____

10. Which shape has six square faces? _____

| Started: | Finished: | Total Time: | Completed: | Correct: |

Name _____   Date _____

Circle the shapes in each row that are not solid shapes.

1.

2.

3.

Match each object with its solid shape. Write the letter for each solid shape on the line next to the object.

4.   _____   A.

5.   _____   B.

6.   _____   C.

7.   _____   D.

Answer the questions about solid shapes.

8. How many round faces does a cone have? _____

9. How many round faces does a cylinder have? _____

10. How many square faces does a cube have? _____

| Started: | Finished: | Total Time: | Completed: | Correct: |

Geometry

Name _____ Date _____

Circle the correct answers.

1. Which solid shape is a sphere? A. ⊕ B. ⬭

2. Which solid shape is a cube? A. △(cone) B. ⬚(cube)

3. Which solid shape is a triangular prism? A. ◿(prism) B. ⬚(cube)

4. Which solid shape is a cylinder? A. ⬚(cube) B. ⬭(cylinder)

5. Which item is a cone?   A. (can) B. (ice cream cone)

Match each "face" to a solid shape.

> A. ◯   B. □   C. △   D. ▭

6. (cube) _____

7. (cylinder) _____

8. (triangular prism) _____ and _____

Name the solid shape for each object.

9. _____   10. _____

Started:	Finished:	Total Time:	Completed:	Correct:

Name _____ Date _____

Look at each shape. Is it divided symmetrically? Circle _Yes_ or _No_.

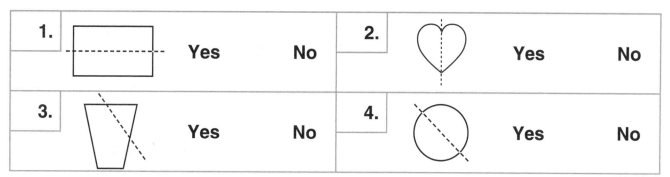

1.	Yes	No	2.	Yes	No
3.	Yes	No	4.	Yes	No

The same object has been divided two ways. Circle the one in each row that is divided symmetrically.

5. A.    B.

6. A.    B.

7. A.    B.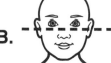

8. A.    B.

9. A.    B.

Divide the domino symmetrically.

10.

Started:	Finished:	Total Time:	Completed:	Correct:

TCR 8081 Timed Math Practice

Name _____ Date _____

Choose the best definition for the word symmetry.

1. _____

A. Both sides of the picture are exactly the same.	B. The line divides the picture in the middle.

Look at the dashed line on each object. Are the two sides symmetrical? Circle *Yes* or *No*.

2.	Yes No	3.	Yes No
4.	Yes No	5.	Yes No

Circle the answer to each question.

6. Which square is divided symmetrically?

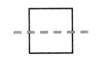 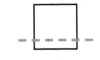

7. Which rectangle is divided symmetrically?

8. Which circle is divided symmetrically?

Divide each triangle symmetrically.

9.   10.

Started:	Finished:	Total Time:	Completed:	Correct:

Name _____ Date _____

**Look at the dashed line on each object. Are the two sides symmetrical?
Circle *Yes* or *No*.**

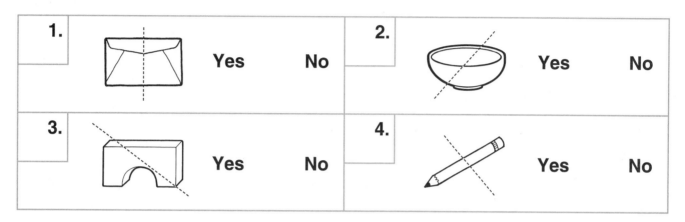

1.	Yes	No	2.	Yes	No
3.	Yes	No	4.	Yes	No

Which circle is divided symmetrically?

5. A.   B.

6. A.   B.

7. A.   B.

8. A.   B.

Divide each rectangle symmetrically.

9.   10.

Started:	Finished:	Total Time:	Completed:	Correct:

Symmetry

Name _____ Date _____

Look at each shape. Does the dashed line make each side symmetrical? Circle *Yes* or *No*.

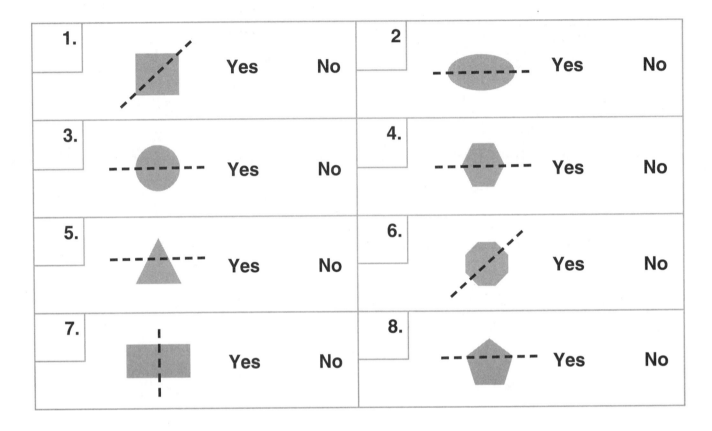

1.	Yes	No
2	Yes	No
3.	Yes	No
4.	Yes	No
5.	Yes	No
6.	Yes	No
7.	Yes	No
8.	Yes	No

Circle the answer to each question.

9. Which hexagon is divided symmetrically?

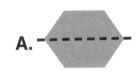   A.

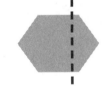   B.

10. Which pentagon is divided symmetrically?

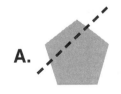   A.

   B.

Started:	Finished:	Total Time:	Completed:	Correct:

Name _____   Date _____

Add the sides to find the perimeters.

1. 3" 3" 3" 3"   _____ + _____ + _____ + _____ = _____"

2. 4" 2" 2" 4"   _____ + _____ + _____ + _____ = _____"

3. 2" 3" 4"   _____ + _____ + _____ = _____"

4. 4" 2" 3" 5"   _____ + _____ + _____ + _____ = _____"

Fill in the missing number for each side.

5. 1" 1" 1" ?   ? = _____"

6. ? 2" 2" 3"   ? = _____"

7. ? 3" 3" 5"   ? = _____"

8. 2" 2" 2" ?   ? = _____"

Solve the word problems. Show your work.

9. Maddox measured a space in his room for his new bed. The rectangle was 3 feet on the short sides and 6 feet on the longer sides. Label the retangle to show this.

10. What was the perimeter of his bed?

_____ + _____ + _____ + _____ = _____

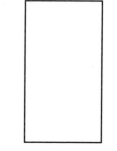

Started:	Finished:	Total Time:	Completed:	Correct:

Perimeter

Name _____ Date _____

Find the perimeter of each triangle.

1. 3" ⟋⟍ 3" 4"   The perimeter is _____ inches.

2. The perimeter is _____ inches. 2" 3" 4"

3. 4" 5" 3"   The perimeter is _____ inches.

4. The perimeter is _____ inches. 6" 6" 4"

5. 3" ⟋⟍ 3" 3"   The perimeter is _____ inches.

Add each side to find the perimeter of each shape.

6. 5" ⟋⟍ 5" 5"   _____ + _____ + _____ = _____"

7. 1" 1" 1" 1" 1" 1"   _____ + _____ + _____ + _____ + _____ + _____ = _____"

8. 3" 3" 3" 3"   _____ + _____ + _____ + _____ = _____"

9. 2" 2" 2" 2" 2"   _____ + _____ + _____ + _____ + _____ = _____"

Solve the word problem. Show your work.

10. Miss Jang went to a soccer game. The field was a very big rectangle.
    It was 100 feet long and 50 feet wide.
    What was the perimeter of the field?

    100 feet
    50 feet

    _____ + _____ + _____ + _____ = _____ **feet**

Started:	Finished:	Total Time:	Completed:	Correct:

 ©*Teacher Created Resources*

Name _____   Date _____

Add the sides to find the perimeter for each shape.

1.   2
      1 /‾‾\ 4   _____ + _____ + _____ + _____ = _____
        3

2.   4
    2 [ ] 2   _____ + _____ + _____ + _____ = _____
      4

3.   3
   ∕‾‾‾\   _____ + _____ + _____ + _____ = _____
  2   2
      5

4.   3 /\ 3   _____ + _____ + _____ + _____ = _____
        3

5.   4 /\ 4
      4 \/ 4   _____ + _____ + _____ + _____ = _____

6.   2
    2 [ ] 2   _____ + _____ + _____ + _____ = _____
      2

Choose the correct answer for each question.

7. How do you find the perimeter of a rectangle?

   A. Add the side and the top.   **B.** Add all four sides.

8. How do you find the perimeter of a square?

   A. Add all four sides.   **B.** Add the top side and the bottom side.

Solve the word problems. Show your work.

9.	Jane's game board is 2 feet on each side. What is the perimeter?
	____ + _____ + _____ + _____ = _____ feet

10.	What is the perimeter of the retangle?
	____ + _____ + _____ + _____ = _____ feet

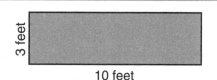

10 feet

Started:	Finished:	Total Time:	Completed:	Correct:

Name _____ Date _____

Look at each circle. Is it divided in half? Answer *Yes* or *No*.

1.		Yes
		No
2.		Yes
		No
3.		Yes
		No
4.		Yes
		No

What is half of each number below?

5. Half of **12** is _____.

6. Half of **20** is _____.

7. Half of **16** is _____.

8. Half of **14** is _____.

Follow the directions for each problem.

9. Count the bells. Circle half of the bells.

10. Count the flowers. Circle half of the flowers.

Started:	Finished:	Total Time:	Completed:	Correct:

Name _____   Date _____

Look at each square. Is it divided in thirds? Answer *Yes* or *No*.

1.   Yes   No

2.   Yes   No

3.   Yes   No

Count the circles. Divide the groups of circles into thirds.

4.   5. ○ ○ ○   6. ○ ○ ○
                                 ○ ○ ○   ○ ○ ○
                                 ○ ○ ○   ○ ○ ○
                                                   ○ ○ ○

Each circle is divided into thirds. Which part is shaded?

7. $\frac{1}{3}$ $\frac{2}{3}$ $\frac{3}{3}$ 8. $\frac{1}{3}$ $\frac{2}{3}$ $\frac{3}{3}$

Solve the word problems. Show your work.

9. | There are three brothers and six cupcakes. If each brother gets the same amount, how many cupcakes does each brother get?

_____ cupcakes

10. | Alan made a pie. When he came home, one third of his pie had been eaten. Which pie shows the missing one third?

A.   B.   C.

| Started: | Finished: | Total Time: | Completed: | Correct: |  |

Fractions

Name _____ Date _____

Look at each shape. Is it divided into equal fourths? Circle *Yes* or *No*.

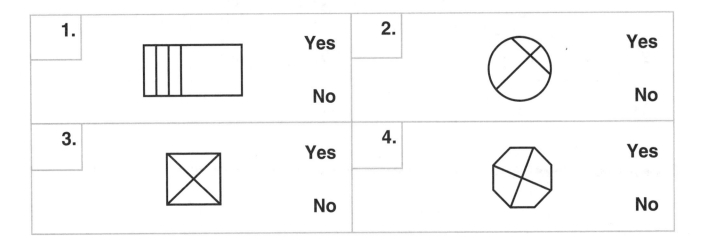

1.   Yes   No

2.   Yes   No

3.   Yes   No

4.   Yes   No

Count each group of crayons. Circle each group of four.

5. _____ groups

6. _____ groups

Shade $\frac{1}{4}$ of each shape.

7.

8.

Divide each rectangle into fourths.

9.

10.

Started:	Finished:	Total Time:	Completed:	Correct:

Name _____ Date _____

Divide each shape in half. Shade one half.

1.   2.   3.   4.

Circle the shape that is divided to match the fraction in the middle.

5. 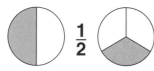 $\frac{1}{2}$ 6. 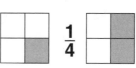 $\frac{1}{4}$ 7. $\frac{2}{3}$

Circle the correct answer to each question.

8. What part of the hexagon is shaded?

$\frac{1}{2}$ $\frac{1}{3}$ $\frac{1}{4}$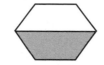

9. What part of the circle is shaded?

$\frac{1}{2}$ $\frac{1}{3}$ $\frac{1}{4}$

10. What part of the rectangle is shaded?

$\frac{1}{2}$ $\frac{1}{3}$ $\frac{1}{4}$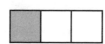

Started:	Finished:	Total Time:	Completed:	Correct:

Name _____ Date _____

Write the number word for each number.

1. 1 _____

2. 10 _____

3. 11 _____

4. 13 _____

Write the following as numbers.

5. twelve _____

6. fifteen _____

7. twenty _____

8. seven _____

Write the correct number and number word for each group of stars.

9. Number _____ Number Word _____

10. Number _____ Number Word _____

Started:	Finished:	Total Time:	Completed:	Correct:

Name _____ Date _____

Write the following as numbers.

1. eighty _____

2. eighteen _____

3. eight _____

4. eighty-eight _____

Write the number word for each number.

5. 43 _____

6. 29 _____

Count the bars and unit cubes. Write the number word for each set of blocks.

7.

8.

_____   _____

Circle the correct number words for each number.

9. | 21 | **two-one**   **twenty**   **twenty-one**

10. | 55 | **fifty**   **fifty-five**   **five-five**

| Started: | Finished: | Total Time: | Completed: | Correct: |

Name _____ Date _____

Write the following as numbers.

1. one hundred twenty-two _____

2. three hundred sixty-five _____

3. nine hundred ninety-nine _____

4. one thousand _____

Chose the correct number words for each number.

		A. five hundred eighty-seven
5.	587 _____	**B.** four hundred eighty-seven
		C. five hundred eight seven

		A. two hundred seven three
6.	273 _____	**B.** two hundred sixty-three
		C. two hundred seventy-three

Write the correct letter for the number word next to each number.

7. 901 _____   **A.** six hundred fifty-eight

8. 658 _____   **B.** nine hundred one

9. 1,000 _____   **C.** six hundred nineteen

10. 619 _____   **D.** one thousand

Started:	Finished:	Total Time:	Completed:	Correct:

Common Core State Standards Correlation

Pages in *Timed Math Practice* meet one or more of the following Common Core State Standards © Copyright 2010. National Governors Association Center for Best Practices and Council of Chief State School Officers. All rights reserved. For more information about the Common Core State Standards, go to *http://www.corestandards. org/* or *http://www.teachercreated.com/standards/.*

Mathematics Standards	Test
Operations and Algebraic Thinking	
Represent and solve problems involving addition and subtraction.	
2.OA.1. Use addition and subtraction within 100 to solve one- and two-step word problems involving situations of adding to, taking from, putting together, taking apart, and comparing, with unknowns in all positions, e.g., by using drawings and equations with a symbol for the unknown number to represent the problem.	11, 13, 18–19, 21–34, 42–48, 50, 54–55, 62–64, 91–93
Add and subtract within 20.	
2.OA.2. Fluently add and subtract within 20 using mental strategies. By end of Grade 2, know from memory all sums of two one-digit numbers.	9, 17–19, 21–32, 34–36, 42–46, 53
Work with equal groups of objects to gain foundations for multiplication.	
2.OA.3. Determine whether a group of objects (up to 20) has an odd or even number of members, e.g., by pairing objects or counting them by 2s; write an equation to express an even number as a sum of two equal addends.	6–7
2.OA.4. Use addition to find the total number of objects arranged in rectangular arrays with up to 5 rows and up to 5 columns; write an equation to express the total as a sum of equal addends.	10–14, 36–41
Number & Operations in Base Ten	
Understand place value.	
2.NBT.1. Understand that the three digits of a three-digit number represent amounts of hundreds, tens, and ones; e.g., 706 equals 7 hundreds, 0 tens, and 6 ones.	10–15, 17
2.NBT.2. Count within 1000; skip-count by 5s, 10s, and 100s.	1–7, 10–14, 17, 36–39
2.NBT.3. Read and write numbers to 1000 using base-ten numerals, number names, and expanded form.	1–7, 10–15, 17, 33, 98–100
2.NBT.4. Compare two three-digit numbers based on meanings of the hundreds, tens, and ones digits, using >, =, and < symbols to record the results of comparisons.	12, 16–20
Use place value understanding and properties of operations to add and subtract.	
2.NBT.5. Fluently add and subtract within 100 using strategies based on place value, properties of operations, and/or the relationship between addition and subtraction.	11, 13, 18–19, 21–35, 42–46, 50–56, 59, 91–93
2.NBT.6. Add up to four two-digit numbers using strategies based on place value and properties of operations.	11, 13, 26–35, 59
2.NBT.7. Add and subtract within 1000, using concrete models or drawings and strategies based on place value, properties of operations, and/or the relationship between addition and subtraction; relate the strategy to a written method. Understand that in adding or subtracting three-digit numbers, one adds or subtracts hundreds and hundreds, tens and tens, ones and ones; and sometimes it is necessary to compose or decompose tens or hundreds.	11, 13, 31–35, 42–52, 54–56, 59, 91–93

2.NBT.8. Mentally add 10 or 100 to a given number 100–900, and mentally subtract 10 or 100 from a given number 100–900.	20
Measurement & Data 2.MD	
2.MD.1. Measure the length of an object by selecting and using appropriate tools such as rulers, yardsticks, meter sticks, and measuring tapes.	57–58, 60–61
2.MD.3. Estimate lengths using units of inches, feet, centimeters, and meters.	57, 60
2.MD.4. Measure to determine how much longer one object is than another, expressing the length difference in terms of a standard length unit.	62–63
Relate addition and subtraction to length.	
2.MD.5. Use addition and subtraction within 100 to solve word problems involving lengths that are given in the same units, e.g., by using drawings (such as drawings of rulers) and equations with a symbol for the unknown number to represent the problem.	58–59, 61–65
2.MD.6. Represent whole numbers as lengths from 0 on a number line diagram with equally spaced points corresponding to the numbers 0, 1, 2, ..., and represent whole-number sums and differences within 100 on a number line diagram.	8–9
Work with time and money.	
2.MD.7. Tell and write time from analog and digital clocks to the nearest five minutes, using a.m. and p.m.	66–71
2.MD.8. Solve word problems involving dollar bills, quarters, dimes, nickels, and pennies, using $ and ¢ symbols appropriately. Example: If you have 2 dimes and 3 pennies, how many cents do you have?	72–77
Represent and interpret data.	
2.MD.10. Draw a picture graph and a bar graph (with single-unit scale) to represent a data set with up to four categories. Solve simple put-together, take-apart, and compare problems using information presented in a bar graph.	78–81
Geometry 2.G	
Reason with shapes and their attributes.	
2.G.1. Recognize and draw shapes having specified attributes, such as a given number of angles or a given number of equal faces. Identify triangles, quadrilaterals, pentagons, hexagons, and cubes.	82–86
2.G.3. Partition circles and rectangles into two, three or four equal shares, describe the shares using the words *halves, thirds, half of, a third of,* etc. and describe the whole as two halves, three thirds, four fourths. Recognize that equal shares of identical wholes need not have the same shape.	94–97

Test 1—Page 5

1. 6
2. 5
3. 8
4. 10
5. 4
6. 9
7. 7
8. 3
9. Third ball should be circled.
10. Fifth ball should be crossed out.

Test 2—Page 6

1. 7
2. 10
3. 9
4. 8
5. 3
6. 6
7. 8
8. 4
9. 9
10. 7

Test 3—Page 7

1. 10
2. 12
3. 8
4. 9
5. 8
6. 11
7. 9
8. 2
9. Tenth ball should be circled.
10. Ninth bat should be circled.

Test 4—Page 8

1. 12
2. 9
3. 11
4. 8
5. 9
6. 12
7. 10
8. 9
9. 13
10. 11

Test 5—Page 9

1. thirteen
2. fourteen
3. fifteen
4. sixteen
5. 13
6. 14
7. 13
8. 8, 9, 10, 11, 12
9. 10, 11, 12, 13, 14
10. 12, 13, 14, 15, 16

Test 6—Page 10

1. seventeen
2. eighteen
3. nineteen
4. twenty
5. 20
6. 18
7. 16
8. 13, 15, 17
9. 13, 19, 11, 15
10. 13, 11, 17, 19

Test 7—Page 11

1. 19
2. 20
3. 17
4. eight
5. thirteen
6. nineteen
7. sixteen
8. 10, 12, 14, 16
9. 20, 16, 14
10. 16, 18, 20

Test 8—Page 12

1. 5
2. 9
3. D
4. A
5. F
6. B
7. E
8. C
9. 14
10. 18

Test 9—Page 13

1. 7
2. 8
3. 10
4. 9
5. 6
6. 8
7. 15
8. 18
9. 19
10. 12

Test 10—Page 14

1. 3 tens + 7 ones = 37
2. 5 tens + 9 ones = 59
3. 1
4. 9
5. 5
6. 3
7. 5
8. 0
9. 9
10. False

Test 11—Page 15

1. 2 tens, 2 ones
2. 6 tens, 5 ones
3. 4 tens, 9 ones
4. 39
5. 65
6. B
7. 60
8. 40
9. 6 tens + 4 ones = 64
10. 8 tens + 0 ones = 80

Test 12—Page 16

1. 2 hundreds 4 tens 6 ones
2. 8 hundreds 9 tens 1 one
3. 5 hundreds 5 tens 2 ones
4. B
5. B
6. A
7. A
8. B
9. 2 hundreds 4 tens 9 ones
10. 2 hundreds 2 tens 2 ones

Test 13—Page 17

1. 476
2. 693
3. 153
4. 3 hundreds 3 tens 3 ones
5. 2 hundreds 5 tens 8 ones
6. 349
7. 675
8. 824
9. 76
10. 500

Test 14—Page 18

1. 611
2. 876
3. 910
4. 875
5. 510
6. 35
7. 3 tens
8. 4 ones
9. 2 tens
10. 234

Test 15—Page 19

1. tens
2. hundreds
3. ones
4. eight hundred fifty-four
5. one hundred eight
6. three hundred ninety-six
7. 441
8. 386
9. 624
10. 809

Test 16—Page 20

1. True
2. False
3. True
4. True
5. 44, 64
6. 113, 133
7. 668, 688
8. <
9. >
10. >

Test 17—Page 21

1. 123 > 113
2. 38 < 42
3. True
4. False
5. False
6. False
7. =
8. <
9. <
10. =

Test 18—Page 22

1. <
2. =
3. >
4. =
5. Michael
6. Jake
7. <
8. >
9. >
10. =

Test 19—Page 23

1. >
2. >
3. <
4. 6 > 5 or 5 < 6
5. Kate
6. False
7. True
8. <
9. <
10. =

Test 20—Page 24

1. 78, 98
2. 146, 166
3. 750, 770
4. 900, 920
5. <
6. =
7. <
8. >
9. 12 < 20 or 20 > 12
10. Tuesday

Test 21—Page 25

1. 9
2. 10
3. 8
4. 9
5. 8
6. 14
7. 18
8. 10
9. 12 + 7 = 19
10. 8 + 6 = 14

Test 22—Page 26

1. 6
2. 5
3. 7
4. 2
5. 4 + 5 = 9
6. 6 + 4 = 10
7. 10
8. 14
9. 14
10. 9

Test 23—Page 27

1. 10
2. 16
3. 7
4. 8
5. 13
6. 14
7. 15
8. 12
9. 16
10. 10 + 4 = 14

Test 24—Page 28

1. 18
2. 15
3. 17
4. 20
5–8. Check the answers.
9. 9 + 11 = 20
10. 13 + 6 = 19

Test 25—Page 29

1. 15
2. 14
3. 17
4. 7
5. 9
6. 5
7. 8
8. 7 + 9 = 16 or 9 + 7 = 16
9. 10 + 3 = 13 or 3 + 10 = 13
10. 9 + 4 = 13 or 4 + 9 + 13

Test 26—Page 30

1. 24
2. 95
3. 49
4. 77
5. 87
6. 80
7. 60
8. 100
9. 50 + 17 = 67
10. 23 + 54 = 77

Test 27—Page 31

1. 23, 65, 11
2. 59, 13, 21
3. 42, 76, 24
4. 86, 62, 34
5. 56
6. 39
7. 86
8. 5
9. 28 + 51 = 79
10. 35 + 62 = 97

Test 28—Page 32

1. 78
2. 74
3. 88
4. 99
5. 99
6. 87
7. 98
8. 50
9. 20
10. 42 + 36 + 11 = 89

Test 29—Page 33

1. 869
2. 859
3. 964
4. 929
5. 445
6. 962
7. 895
8. 992
9. 125 + 342 = 467
10. 200 + 175 = 375

Test 30—Page 34

1. 661
2. 795
3. 778
4. 431
5. 789
6. 887
7. 939
8. 779
9. 251 + 327 = 578
10. 425 + 432 = 857

Test 31—Page 35

1. 100
2. 41
3. 71
4. 64
5. 81
6. 92
7. 100
8. 36 + 48 = 84
9. 25 + 34 + 21 = 80
10. 36 + 34 = 70

Test 32—Page 36

1. 85 + 60 = 145 inches
2. 59 + 86 = 145 inches
3. 86 + 85 = 171 inches
4. 85 + 60 = 145 inches
5. 61 + 59 = 120 inches
6. 85 + 61 = 146 inches
7. 144 inches
8. Mary
9. Casey
10. Luke and James

Test 33—Page 37

1. 8
2. 9
3. 5
4. 410
5. 719
6. 990
7. 824
8. 580
9. 127 + 184 = 311
10. 495 + 232 = 727

Test 34—Page 38

1. 96 + 96 = 192
2. 365 + 365 = 730
3. 800
4. 700
5. 631
6. 910
7. 580
8. 681
9. 993
10. 394

Test 35—Page 39

1. 790
2. 110
3. 851
4. 831
5. 830
6. 200
7. 200
8. 400
9. 316
10. 470

Test 36—Page 40

1. 2, **4**, 6, **8**, 10
2. 6, **8**, 10, 12,**14**
3. 4, **6**, **8**, 10, 12
4. 8
5. 10
6. 16
7. 10; 2 × 5 = 10
8. 14; 2 × 7 = 14
9. 18; 2 × 9 = 18
10. 16; 2 × 8 = 16

Test 37—Page 41

1. 3, **6**, 9, **12**, 15
2. 6, **9**, 12, **15**, 18
3. 9, **12**, 15, **18**, 21
4. 9
5. 18
6. 15
7. 12; 3 × 4 = 12
8. 15; 3 × 5 = 15
9. 18; 3 × 6 = 18
10. 21; 3 × 7 = 21

Answer Key (cont.)

Test 38—Page 42
1. 5, 10, **15**, 20, **25**
2. 10, **15**, **20**, 25, 30
3. 15, **20**, 25, **30**, 35
4. 10
5. 20
6. 15
7. 30; 5 × 6 = 30
8. 45; 5 × 9 = 45
9. 35; 5 × 7 = 35
10. 50; 5 × 10 = 50

Test 39—Page 43
1. 10, **20**, 30, **40**
2. 30, **40**, **50**, 60
3. 40, **50**, 60, **70**, 80
4. 50, 60, **70**, 80, **90**
5. 40
6. 70
7. 60; 6 × 10 = 60
8. 80; 8 × 10 = 80
9. 70; 7 × 10 = 70
10. 100; 10 × 10 = 100

Test 40—Page 44
1. 2 + 2 + 2 + 2 + 2 + 2 = 12
2. 2 × 6 = 12
3. 2 + 2 + 2 + 2 = 8
4. 2 × 4 = 8
5. 2 + 2 + 2 + 2 + 2 + 2 + 2 = 14
6. 2 × 7 = 14
7. 3 + 3 = 6
8. 2 × 3 = 6
9. 3 + 3 + 3 + 3 = 12
10. 3 × 4 = 12

Test 41—Page 45
1. 5 + 5 + 5 + 5 = 20
2. 5 × 4 = 20
3. 5 + 5 + 5 + 5 + 5 + 5 = 30
4. 5 × 6 = 30
5. 5 + 5 + 5 + 5 + 5 + 5 + 5 + 5 = 40
6. 5 × 8 = 40
7. 5 + 5 + 5 = 15
8. 3 × 5 = 15
9. 5 + 5 + 5 + 5 + 5 = 25
10. 5 × 5 = 25

Test 42—Page 46
1. 3
2. 7
3. 3
4. 7
5. 6
6. 13
7. 6
8. 14
9. 12 − 7 = 5 or 12 − 5 = 7
10. 18 − 9 = 9

Test 43—Page 47
1. 9
2. 12
3. 5
4. 16
5. 8
6. 4
7. 9
8. 17 − 8 = 9 or 17 − 9 = 8
9. 11 − 4 = 7 or 11 − 7 = 4
10. 15 − 9 = 6 ; 6

Test 44—Page 48
1. 7
2. 7
3. 5
4. 9
5. 7
6. 9
7. 8
8. 10
9. 16 − 7 = 9 or 16 − 9 = 7
10. 14 − 8 = 6 or 14 − 6 = 8

Test 45—Page 49
1. 11
2. 13
3. 12
4. 80
5. 40
6. 20
7. 21
8. 13
9. 21
10. 89 − 16 = 73

Test 46—Page 50
1. 31
2. 32
3. 44
4. 12
5. $87 − $53 = $34
6. $99 − $48 = $51
7. 27
8. 21
9. 54
10. 43

Test 47—Page 51
1. 111
2. 130
3. 522
4. 132
5. 401
6. 13
7. 300
8. 200
9. 100
10. 244 − 122 = 122

Test 48—Page 52
1. 123
2. 424
3. 24
4. 311
5. 930
6. 420
7. 700
8. 310
9. 458 − 237 = 221
10. 600 − 200 = 400

Test 49—Page 53
1. 120
2. 340
3. 530
4. 200
5. 131
6. 102
7. 135
8. 113
9. 2
10. 3

Test 50—Page 54
1. 45
2. 9
3. 38
4. 6
5. 14
6. 25
7. 80
8. 12
9. 25 − 16 = 9
10. 24 − 16 = 8

Test 51—Page 55
1. 18
2. 9
3. 18
4. 19
5. 153
6. 89
7. 60
8. 67
9. 14
10. 98

Test 52—Page 56
1. 99
2. 444
3. 180
4. 154
5. 3
6. 6
7. 75
8. 50
9. 25
10. 50

Test 53—Page 57
1. 13
2. 13
3. 6
4. 7
5. −
6. +
7. −
8. +
9. 94
10. 33

Test 54—Page 58
1. 66
2. 786
3. 31
4. 133
5. +
6. −
7. +
8. +
9. 20 + 20 + 20 = 60
10. 45 − 15 = 30

Test 55—Page 59

1. +
2. –
3. –
4. +
5. 17
6. 76
7. 200
8. 17
9. 230 – 45 = 185; 185
10. 83 – 17 = 66; 66

Test 56—Page 60

1. 810
2. 900
3. 830
4. 760
5. 18
6. 199
7. 49
8. 108
9. 100 – 53 = 47
10. 324 + 259 = 583

Test 57—Page 61

1. B
2. B
3. A
4. A
5. 2
6. 3
7. False
8. True
9. False
10. True

Test 58—Page 62

1. 4
2. 5
3. A
4. 4 feet
5. 3 feet
6. 9 feet
7. 8 feet
8. frog
9. kangaroo
10. 4 – 3 = 1 foot

Test 59—Page 63

1. 30
2. 10 + 40 = 50
3. Monday
4. Tuesday and Friday
5. 20 + 40 = 60
6. 10 + 40 + 30 = 80
7. 40 + 40 = 80
8. 78
9. 57
10. 70

Test 60—Page 64

1. 6
2. 10
3. 5
4. 16
5. meters
6. centimeters
7. meters
8. centimeters
9. 8
10. 7

Test 61—Page 65

1. 10
2. 6
3. 5
4. 3
5. 10 cm
6. 11 cm
7. 14 cm
8. 8 cm
9. 3 cm
10. 5 cm

Test 62—Page 66

1. B
2. C
3. 75 + 100 = 175 ft.
4. 75 + 100+ 50 = 225 ft.
5. 100 – 50 = 50 ft.
6. 100 – 75 = 25 ft.
7. horse
8. bus
9. inch
10. 18 + 14 = 32

Test 63—Page 67

1. C
2. B
3. A and D
4. True
5. True
6. False
7. True
8. 2
9. 5
10. 18

Test 64—Page 68

1. True
2. False
3. True
4. 4
5. 7
6. 3
7. A
8. B
9. 5 + 8 = 13
10. 12 + 8 = 20

Test 65—Page 69

1. No
2. Yes
3. Yes
4. No
5. Yes
6. 50 lbs.
7. 18 lbs.
8. 68 lbs.
9. 67 lbs.
10. 88 lbs.

Test 66—Page 70

1. 2:00
2. 4:15
3. 7:30
4. 10:45
5. 10:15
6. 2:45
7. 5:15

8.
9.
10. True

Test 67—Page 71

1. two thirty
2. twelve fifteen
3. seven thirty
4. 3:15

5. 5:15
6. 8:30
7. 12:30
8. 7:50
9. 4:20
10. 8:45

Test 68—Page 72

1. 6:05
2. 11:35
3. 3:55
4. 10:40

5.
6.
7.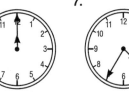

8.
9.
10. 12:40

Test 69—Page 73

1. 1:20; 4:20
2. 11:40; 2:40
3. 10:10; 1:10
4. 2:00
5. 9:45
6. 8:15

7.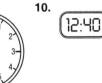
9.
8. 6:25
10. 9:45

Test 70—Page 74

1. 7 p.m.
2. 3:30
3. True
4. False
5. True
6. True

7. 10:10
8. 10:15
9. 11:00
10. 10:20

Test 71—Page 75

1. C
2. A
3. B
4. D
5. 2:40
6.

7.
8. 12:10
9. 5:40
10. 3:35

Test 72—Page 76

1. quarter
2. penny
3. nickel
4. dime
5. 1¢

6. 25¢
7. 10¢
8. 5¢
9. 5
10. 10

Test 73—Page 77

1. 25
2. 2
3. 5
4. 100
5. 20

6. 10
7. 4
8. 25
9. 28
10. 100

Test 74—Page 78

1. 75¢ or $0.75
2. $1.00 or 100¢
3. 50¢ or $0.50
4. $1.50 or 150¢
5. 30¢ or $0.30

6. 60¢ or $0.60
7. 90¢ or $0.90
8. 41¢ or $0.41
9. 35¢ or $0.35
10. 90¢ or $0.90

Test 75—Page 79

1. $3.00
2. $6.00
3. $4.00
4. 2, 5
5. 3, 3

6. 2, 2, 2
7. $2.50
8. $1.77
9. $4.15
10. $2.20

Test 76—Page 80

1. 65
2. 99
3. 185
4. $1.66
5. $1.16
6. $1.11

7.
8.
9.
10.

Test 77—Page 81

1. =
2. <
3. >
4. >

5. 50¢
6. 35¢
7. 55¢
8.

9.
10.

Test 78—Page 82

1. soccer
2. basketball
3. 7
4. 12
5. 5

6. 9
7. 8
8. 10
9. 8 + 9 = 17
10. 10 + 9 = 19

Test 79—Page 83

1. 13
2. 10
3. 20
4. 7
5. Car 4

6. Car 3
7. boat
8. jet
9. 20
10. 20 − 10 = 10

Test 80—Page 84

1. peach
2. 8
3. banana
4. 6
5. 14 − 10 = 4

6. 6 + 8 = 14
7. IIII
8. NN NN
9. NN NN NN II
10. NN NN NN NN III

Test 81—Page 85

1. 13
2. 8
3. 12
4. 6
5. 15

6. 8 + 6 = 14
7. 12 − 6 = 6
8. 12 + 6 = 18
9. 15 + 12 = 27
10. 13 − 8 = 5

Test 82—Page 86

1. rectangle
2. square
3. triangle
4. rhombus
5. oval

6. triangle
7. rectangle
8. rhombus
9. square or rhombus
10. C

Test 83—Page 87

1. octagon
2. hexagon
3. pentagon
4. hexagon
5. octagon

6. pentagon
7. oval
8. rectangle
9. circle
10. 2 triangles

Test 84—Page 88

1. cylinder
2. sphere
3. cube
4. prism
5. cone

6. prism
7. cylinder and cone
8. sphere
9. cylinder
10. cube

Test 85—Page 89

1. circle and triangle
2. square and circle
3. rectangle and triangle
4. C
5. D

6. B
7. A
8. 1
9. 2
10. 6

Test 86—Page 90

1. A
2. B
3. A
4. B
5. B

6. B
7. A
8. C and D
9. cube
10. sphere

Test 87—Page 91
1. Yes
2. Yes
3. No
4. Yes
5. B
6. A
7. A
8. B
9. B
10. Check answer.

Test 88—Page 92
1. A
2. Yes
3. Yes
4. No
5. No
6. Check the answers.
7. Check the answers.
8. Check the answers.
9. Check the dividing line.
10. Check the dividing line.

Test 89—Page 93
1. Yes
2. No
3. No
4. No
5. B
6. A
7. B
8. B
9. Check dividing line.
10. Check dividing line.

Test 90—Page 94
1. Yes
2. Yes
3. Yes
4. Yes
5. No
6. Yes
7. Yes
8. No
9. A
10. B

Test 91—Page 95
1. 3 + 3 + 3 + 3 = 12
2. 2 + 4 + 2 + 4 = 12
3. 2 + 3 + 4 = 9
4. 2 + 4 + 3 + 5 = 14
5. 1
6. 3
7. 5
8. 2
9. Check the labels.
10. 3 + 6 + 3 + 6 = 18

Test 92—Page 96
1. 10
2. 9
3. 12
4. 16
5. 9
6. 5 + 5 + 5 = 15
7. 1 + 1 + 1 + 1 + 1 + 1 = 6
8. 3 + 3 + 3 + 3 = 12
9. 2 + 2 + 2 + 2 + 2 = 10
10. 100 + 50 + 100 + 50 = 300

Test 93—Page 97
1. 2 + 3 + 4 + 1 = 10
2. 2 + 4 + 2 + 4 = 12
3. 5 + 2 + 3 + 2 = 12
4. 3 + 3 + 3 = 9
5. 4 + 4 + 4 + 4 = 16
6. 2 + 2 + 2 + 2 = 8
7. B
8. A
9. 2 + 2 + 2 + 2 = 8
10. 3 + 10 + 3 + 10 = 26

Test 94—Page 98
1. Yes
2. Yes
3. No
4. Yes
5. 6
6. 10
7. 8
8. 7
9. 7 bells should be circled
10. 9 flowers should be circled

Test 95—Page 99
1. Yes
2. No
3. Yes
4. Check the groups.
5. Check the groups.
6. Check the groups.
7. 1/3
8. 2/3
9. 2 cupcakes
10. B

Test 96—Page 100
1. No
2. No
3. Yes
4. Yes
5. 3 groups of 4 crayons
6. 2 groups of 4 crayons
7. Check the shading.
8. Check the shading.
9. Check the dividing lines. 3 groups
10. Check the dividing lines. 2 groups

Test 97—Page 101
1. Check the shading.
2. Check the shading.
3. Check the shading.
4. Check the shading.
5.
6.
7.
8. 1/2
9. 1/4
10. 1/3

Test 98—Page 102
1. one
2. ten
3. eleven
4. thirteen
5. 12
6. 15
7. 20
8. 7
9. 18; eighteen
10. 14; fourteen

Test 99—Page 103
1. 80
2. 18
3. 8
4. 88
5. forty-three
6. twenty-nine
7. eighty-one
8. sixty-seven
9. twenty-one
10. fifty-five

Test 100—Page 104
1. 122
2. 365
3. 999
4. 1,000
5. A. five hundred eighty-seven
6. C. two hundred seventy-three
7. B
8. A
9. D
10. C